Books and Bookmen [Essays]

WORKS BY THE SAME AUTHOR.

ANGLING SKETCHES. With Illustrations by W. G. BURN-MURDOCH. Crown 8vo. *7s. 6d.*

CUSTOM AND MYTH: Studies of Early Usage and Belief. With 15 Illustrations. Crown 8vo. *7s. 6d.*

GRASS OF PARNASSUS. A Volume of Verses.

BALLADS OF BOOKS. Edited by ANDREW LANG. Fcap. 8vo. *6s.*

LETTERS TO DEAD AUTHORS. Crown 8vo. *2s. 6d. net.*

BOOKS AND BOOKMEN. With 2 Coloured Plates and 17 Illustrations. Crown 8vo. *2s. 6d. net.*

LETTERS ON LITERATURE.

OLD FRIENDS: Essays in Epistolary Parody.

THE BLUE FAIRY BOOK. Edited by ANDREW LANG. With 8 Plates and 130 Illustrations in the Text. Crown 8vo. *6s.*

THE RED FAIRY BOOK. Edited by ANDREW LANG. With 4 Plates and 96 Illustrations in the Text. Crown 8vo. *6s.*

THE BLUE POETRY BOOK. Edited by ANDREW LANG. With 12 Plates and 88 Illustrations in the Text. Crown 8vo. *6s.*

LONDON: LONGMANS, GREEN, & CO.

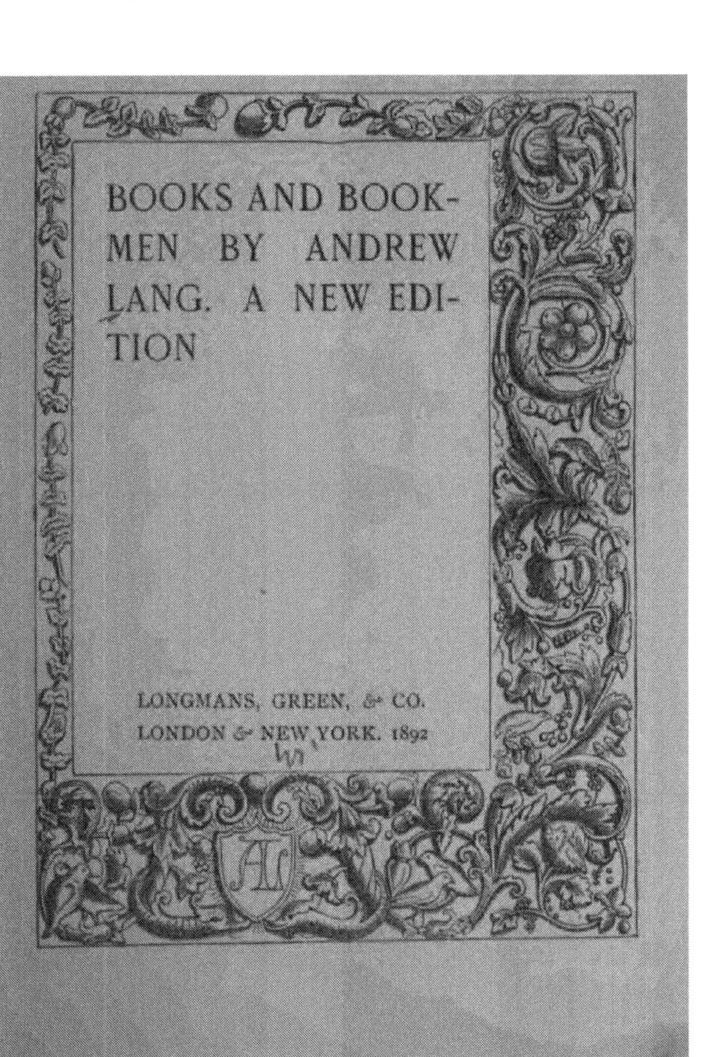

BOOKS AND BOOKMEN BY ANDREW LANG. A NEW EDITION

LONGMANS, GREEN, & CO.
LONDON & NEW YORK. 1892

TO

THE VISCOUNTESS WOLSELEY

MADAME, it is no modish thing,
The bookman's tribute that I bring;
A talk of antiquaries grey,
Dust unto dust this many a day,
Gossip of texts and bindings old,
Of faded type, and tarnish'd gold!

Can ladies care for this to-do
With Payne, Derome, and Padeloup?
Can they resign the rout, the ball,
For lonely joys of shelf and stall?

The critic thus, serenely wise;
But you can read with other eyes,
Whose books and bindings treasured are
'Midst mingled spoils of peace and war;
Shields from the fights the Mahdi lost,
And trinkets from the Golden Coast,
And many a thing divinely done
By Chippendale and Sheraton,

And trophies of Egyptian deeds,
And fans, and plates, and Aggrey beads,
Pomander boxes, assegais,
And sword-hilts worn in Marlbro's days.

In this abode of old and new,
Of war and peace, my essays, too,
For long in serials tempest-tost,
Are landed now, and are not lost:
Nay, on your shelf secure they lie,
As in the amber sleeps the fly.
'Tis true, they are not "rich nor rare;"
Enough, for me, that they are—there!

A. L.

PREFACE

THE Essays in this volume have, for the most part, already appeared in an American edition (Combes, New York, 1886). The Essays on "Old French Title-Pages" and "Lady Book-Lovers" take the place of "Book Binding" and "Bookmen at Rome;" "Elzevirs" and "Some Japanese Bogie-Books" are reprinted, with permission of Messrs. Cassell, from the *Magazine of Art;* "Literary Forgeries" from the *Contemporary Review;* "Lady Book-Lovers" from the *Fortnightly Review;* "A Bookman's Purgatory" and two of the pieces of verse from *Longman's Magazine*—with the courteous permission of the various editors. All the chapters have been revised, and I have to thank Mr. H. Tedder for his kind care in reading the proof sheets.

The Author learns, on the best authority, that the modern flat-backed bindings, referred to on p. 175, line 7, are well supplied with *nerfs*, though these do not show, and are perfectly permanent. The artistic and traditional objection to flat, still more to hollow backs, is another question.

As the reference on p. 155 is intended to show, "A Bookman's Purgatory" is adapted from a little volume, now rather rare, "L'Enfer d'un Bibliophile," by the late M. Charles Asselinean.

CONTENTS

ILLUSTRATIONS

AND BOOKMEN.

ELZEVIRS.

"You know how much, for
past, the editions of the Elzevirs
demand. The fancy for them
penetrated into the country. I am
with a man there who denies himself
for the sake of collecting into a
where other books are scarce enough)
little Elzevirs as he can lay his hands
He is dying of hunger, and his conso-
be able to say, 'I have all the poets
Elzevirs printed. I have ten examples
them, all with red letters, and all of
date.' This, no doubt, is a craze, for,
books are, if he kept them to read
example of each would be enough."
If he had wanted to read
have advised him to buy
of minor authors which

these booksellers published, even editions [illegible] the right date,' as you say, are not too correct. Nothing is good in the books but the type and the paper. Your friend would have done better to use the editions of Gryphius or Estienne."

This fragment of a literary dialogue I translate from "Entretiens sur les Contes de Fées," a book which contains more of old talk about books and booksellers than about fairies and folk-lore. The "Entretiens" were published in 1699, about sixteen years after the Elzevirs ceased to be publishers. The fragment is valuable: first, because it shows us how early the taste for collecting Elzevirs was fully developed; and, secondly, because it contains very sound criticism of the mania. Already, in the seventeenth century, lovers of the tiny Elzevirian books waxed pathetic over dates, already they knew that a "Cæsar" of 1635 was the right "Cæsar," already they were fond of the red-lettered passages, as in the first edition of the "Virgil" of 1636. As early as 1699, too, the Parisian critic knew that the editions were not [illegible] correct, and that the paper, type, ornaments, and *format* were their main attractions. [illegible] must now add the rarity of really good [illegible]

Though Elzevirs have been [illegible] than at present, they are still [illegible] novelists as the great prize of the book collector. You read in novels about "priceless little Elzevirs," about books "as rare as an old Elzevir." I have met, in the works of a lady novelist (but not elsewhere), with an Elzevir "Theocritus." The late Mr. Hepworth Dixon introduced into one of his romances a romantic Elzevir Greek Testament, "worth its weight in gold." Casual remaιks of this kind encourage

a popular delusion that all Elzevirs are pearls of considerable price. When a man is first smitten with the pleasant fever of book-collecting, it is for Elzevirs that he searches. At first he thinks himself in amazing luck. In Booksellers' Row and in Castle Street he "picks up," for a shilling or two, Elzevirs, real or supposed. To the beginner, any book with a sphere on the title-page is an Elzevir. For the beginner's instruction, two copies of spheres are printed here. The first is a sphere, an ill-cut, ill-drawn sphere, which is not Elzevirian at all. The mark was used in the seventeenth century by many other booksellers and printers. The second, on the other hand, is a true Elzevirian sphere, from a play of Molière's, printed in 1675. Observe the comparatively neat drawing of the second sphere, and be not led away after spurious imitations.

Beware, too, of the vulgar error of fancying that little duodecimos with the mark of the fox and the bee's nest, and the motto "Quaerendo," come from the press of the Elzevirs. The mark is that of Abraham Wolfgang, which name is not a pseudonym for Elzevir. There are three sorts of Elzevir pseudonyms. First, they occasionally reprinted the full title-page, publisher's name and all, of the book they pirated. Secondly, when they printed books of a "dangerous" sort, Jansenist pamphlets and so forth, they used pseudonyms like "Nic. Schouten," on the "Lettres Provinciales" of Pascal. Thirdly, there are real pseudonyms employed by the Elzevirs. John and Daniel, printing at L[illegible] (1652–1655), used the false name "Jean S[illegible] The Elzevirs of Amsterdam often [illegible] name "Jacques le Jeune" on their [illegible] The collector who remembers these [illegible]

[illegible] have the right orna- [illegible] chapters, the right tail- [illegible]. Two of the most frequently [illegible] are the so-called "Tête de [illegible] Sirène." More or less clumsy [illegible] and the other Elzevirian orna- [illegible] enough in books of the [illegible] among those printed out of the [illegible]; for example, in books published [illegible]

[illegible] of the history of the Elzevirs [illegible]. The founder of the family, [illegible] bookbinder, Louis, left Louvain and [illegible] in 1580. He bought a house [illegible] University, and opened a book- [illegible] shop, on college ground, was [illegible]. Louis was a good bookseller, [illegible] publisher. It was not till [illegible] his death, in 1617, that his [illegible] bought a set of types and other [illegible] left six sons. Two of these, [illegible] Bonaventure, kept on the business, [illegible] *Elzeviriana*. In 1625 Bona- [illegible] (son of Matthew) became [illegible] good "dates" of Elzevirian [illegible]. The two Elzevirs chose [illegible] nine years' endeavours [illegible] "Cæsar" of 1635.

Their classical series in *petit format* ... opened with "Horace" and "Ovid" in ... In 1641 they began their elegant ... French plays and poetry with "Le Cid." It ... worth while being pirated by the Elzevirs, ... turned you out like a gentleman, with ... and red letters, and a pretty frontispiece. The modern pirate dresses you in rags, prints ... murderously, and binds you, if he binds you at all, in some hideous example of "cloth extra," all gilt, like archaic gingerbread. Bonaventure and Abraham both died in 1652. They did not depart before publishing (1628), in *grand format*, a desirable work on fencing, Thibault's "Académie de l'Espée." This Tibbald ... killed by the book. John and Daniel Elzevir came next. They brought out the "Imitation" (Thomæ a Kempis canonici regularis ord. S. Augustini De Imitatione Christi, libri iv) ... wish by taking thought I could add eight milli-metres to the stature of my copy. In ... Daniel joined a cousin, Louis, in Amsterdam, and John stayed in Leyden. John died ... his widow struggled on, but her son, A... (1681) let all fall into ruins. A... 1712. The Elzevirs of Amsterdam ... 1680, when Daniel died, and ... wound up. The type ...

THOMÆ A KEMPIS
CANONICI REGVLARIS
ORD. S. AVGVSTINI
DE IMITATIONE
CHRISTI
Libri Quatuor.
LVGDVNI
Apud Joh. et Dan. Elsevirios

Dyck, was sold in 1681, by Daniel's [illegible]
Sic transit gloria.

After he has learned all these matters [illegible] amateur has still a great deal to acquire. [illegible] may now know a real Elzevir from a book [illegible] is not an Elzevir at all. But there are enormous differences of value, rarity, and excellence among the productions of the Elzevirian press. The bookstalls teem with small, "cropped," dingy, dirty, battered Elzevirian editions of the classics, *not* "of the good date." On these it is not worth while to expend a couple of shillings, especially as Elzevirian type is too small to be read with comfort by most modern eyes. No, let the collector save his money; avoid littering his shelves with what he will soon find to be rubbish, and let him wait the chance of acquiring a really beautiful and rare Elzevir.

Meantime, and before we come to describe Elzevirs of the first flight, let it be remembered that the "taller" the copy, the less harried and nipped by the binder's shears, the better. "Men scarcely know how beautiful fire is," says Shelley, and we may say that most men hardly [illegible] how beautiful an Elzevir was in its [illegible] original form. The Elzevirs we have [illegible] "dear," but they are certainly "dumpy" [illegible] Their fair proportions have been [illegible]

[illegible] sale there was a pearl
[illegible] Marot, — not an Elzevir, indeed,
[illegible] published by Wetstein, a follower of
[illegible] This exquisite pair of volumes,
[illegible] morocco, was absolutely un-
[illegible] and was a sight to bring happy tears
[illegible] eyes of the amateur of Elzevirs. There
[illegible] elegance about these tomes;
[illegible] and exquisite delicacy of propor-
[illegible] linger like sweet music in the memory.
[illegible] copy of the Wetstein "Marot" myself,
[illegible] copy, though murderously bound in
[illegible] sort of brown calf antique,
[illegible] well with hymn books, and reminds
[illegible] of chocolate. But my copy is only
[illegible] millimetres in height, whereas the
[illegible] copy (it had belonged to the
[illegible]) was at least 130 millimetres
[illegible] the uncut example mine looks like
[illegible] plain sister beside the beauty of the
[illegible]

[illegible] moral is that only tall Elzevirs are
[illegible] tall Elzevirs preserve their
[illegible], only tall Elzevirs are worth
[illegible] Lemuel Gulliver remarks that
[illegible] was taller than any of his
[illegible] breadth of a nail, and that
[illegible] minds of all with awe.

Well, the Philistine may think a few
more or less, in the height of an
little importance. When he comes
will discover the difference. An uncut,
uncut, copy of a good Elzevir may
fifty or sixty pounds or more; an
may bring fewer pence. The binders
pare down the top and bottom more
sides. I have a "Rabelais" of the
with the red title (1663), and some of the
have never been opened, at the sides.
height is only some 122 millimetres,
dwarf. Anything over 130 millimetres
rare. Therefore the collector of Elzevirs
have one of those useful ivory-handled
on which the French measures are marked,
thus he will at once be able to satisfy
to the exact height of any example which
encounters.

Let us now assume that the amateur
understands what a proper Elzevir should
tall, clean, well bound if possible, and
good date. But we have still to learn
good dates are, and this is matter for
and practice of a well-spent life.
gossip about a few of the more famous
those without which no collection
Of all Elzevirs the most famous

expensive is an old cookery book, "'Le Pastissier François.' Wherein is taught the way to make all sorts of pastry, useful to all sorts of persons. Also the manner of preparing all manner of eggs, for fast-days, and other days, in more than sixty fashions. Amsterdam, Louys, and Daniel Elsevier. 1665." The mark is not the old "Sage," but the "Minerva" with her owl. Now this book has no intrinsic value any more than

a Tauchnitz reprint of any modern volume on cooking. The "Pastissier" is cherished because it is so very rare. The tract passed into the hands of cooks, and the hands of cooks are detrimental to literature. Just as nursery books, fairy tales, and the like are destroyed from generation to generation, so it happens with books used in the kitchen. The "Pastissier," to be sure, has a good frontispiece, a scene in a Low Country kitchen, among the dead game and the dainties. The buxom cook [illegible] a game pie; a pheasant pie, decorated [illegible] bird's head and tail-feathers, is already [illegible]

Not for these charms, but for its rarity, [illegible] "Pastissier" coveted. In an early edition [illegible] "Manuel" (1821) Brunet says, with a [illegible] brutality (for he dearly loved an Elzevir), [illegible] now I have disdained to admit this book [illegible] my work, but I have yielded to the prayers [illegible] amateurs. Besides, how could I keep [illegible] volume which was sold for one hundred and [illegible] francs in 1819?" One hundred and one [illegible] If I could only get a "Pastissier" for [illegible] hundred and one francs! But our grandfa[illegible] lived in the Bookman's Paradise. "Il n'est [illegible] jusqu'aux Anglais," adds Brunet—"the [illegible] English themselves—have a taste for the '[illegible] tissier.'" The Duke of Marlborough's copy [illegible] actually sold for £1 4*s*. It would have [illegible] money in the ducal pockets of the house [illegible] Marlborough to have kept this volume till [illegible] general sale of all their portable property [illegible] which our generation was privileged to [illegible] No wonder the "Pastissier" was thought [illegible] Bérard only knew two copies. Pieters, [illegible] on the Elzevirs in 1843, could [illegible] "Pastissiers," and in his "Annales" [illegible]

[1] See illustration, [illegible]

[illegible] but five more. Willems, on the other [illegible] enumerates some thirty, not including [illegible]'s. Motteley was an uncultivated, un[illegible] enthusiast. He knew no Latin, but he [illegible] fair for uncut Elzevirs. "Incomptis [illegible]," he would cry (it was all his lore) as he [illegible] over his treasures. They were all burnt [illegible] Commune in the Louvre Library.

[illegible] examples may be given of the prices [illegible] by "Le Pastissier" in later days. [illegible] copy was but 128 millimetres in [illegible] and had the old ordinary vellum bind[illegible] fact, it closely resembled a copy which [illegible] Ellis and White had for sale in Bond [illegible] 1883. The English booksellers asked, [illegible] about 1500 francs for their copy. [illegible] was sold for 128 francs in April, 1828; [illegible] francs in 1837. Then the book was [illegible] bound by Trautz-Bauzonnet, and [illegible] with Potier's books in 1870, when it [illegible] francs. At the Benzon sale (1875) [illegible] francs, and, falling dreadfully in [illegible] sold again in 1877 for 2200 francs. [illegible] Rosen, has a taller copy, bound [illegible] Last time it was sold (1851) it [illegible]. The Duc de Chartres has [illegible] Pieters, the historian of the [illegible] francs.

About thirty years ago no fewer th
copies were sold at Brighton, of
M. Quentin Bauchart had a copy
millimetres in height, which he
M. Paillet. M. Chartener, of Metz, had
now bound by Bauzonnet which was
four francs in 1780. We call this the
cheap books, but before the Revolution
were cheaper. It is fair to say, however
this example of the "Pastissier" was
bound up with another book, Vlacq's edition
"Le Cuisinier François," and so went che
than it would otherwise have done. M.
Fontaine de Resbecq declares that a friend
his bought six original pieces of Molière
bound up with an old French translation
Garth's "Dispensary." The one faint
left to the poor book collector is that he
find a valuable tract lurking in the leaves
some bound collection of trash. I have
original copy of Molière's "Les Fâcheux"
bound up with a treatise on precious
but the bookseller from whom I bought it
it was there! That made all the difference

But, to return to our "Pastissier,"
M. de Fontaine de Resbecq's account
wooed and won his own copy of the
Elzevir. "I began my walk

... stalls, by the Pont Marie
... de la Grève, the pillars of
... of the bookhunting world. After
... viewed and reviewed these remote books,
... going away, when my attention was
... by a small naked volume, without a
... binding. I seized it, and what was
... when I recognised one of the rarest
... Elzevir collection whose height is
... as minutely as the carats of the
... There was no indication of price on
... where this jewel was lying; the book,
... unbound, was perfectly clean within.
... ?' said I to the bookseller. 'You
... it for six sous,' he answered; 'is it too
... 'No,' said I, and, trembling a little, I
... the thirty centimes he asked for
... François.' You may believe,
... that after such a piece of luck at the
... goes home fondly embracing the
... of one's search. That is exactly

... be true? Is such luck given by
... *mortalibus aegris?* M. de
... made apparently in 1856,
... plenty in the streams, and
... rate. To my own know-
... collector has bought an

original play of Molière's, in the original ... for eighteenpence. But no one has ... any longer. Not, at least, in London. ... expensive "Pastissier" than that which ... six sous was priced in Bachelin-Deflorenne's catalogue at £240. A curious thing ... when two uncut "Pastissiers" turned up ... taneously in Paris. One of them Morgand ... Fatout sold for £400. Clever people ... that one of the twin uncut "Pastissiers" ... be an imitation, a fac-simile by means of ... gravure, or some other process. But it ... triumphantly established that both were genuine ... they had minute points of difference in ... ornaments.

M. Willems, the learned historian of ... Elzevirs, is indignant at the successes of a ... which, as Brunet declares, is badly printed ... There must be at least forty known "Pastissiers" ... in the world. Yes; but there are, at ... 4000 people who would greatly rejoice ... possess a "Pastissier," and some of these ... sirous ones are very wealthy. While this ... of the market endures, the "Pastissier" ... fetch higher prices than the other ... Another extremely rare Elzevir is ... Théâtre de Mons. Corneille" ... This contains "Le Cid," "Les ...

[illegible] "Le Polyeucte,"
[illegible] Théâtre," appearing at
[illegible] of his own. In 1643-44,
[illegible] Madeleine Béjart had just started
[illegible] which they called "L'Illustre
[illegible] Only six or seven copies of the
[illegible] known, though three or four
[illegible] to exist in England, probably all
[illegible] dust in the library of some lord.
[illegible] a very good library," I once heard
[illegible] say to a noble earl, whose own library
[illegible] "And what can a fellow do with
[illegible] library?" answered the descendant
[illegible] who probably (being a youth
[illegible] and content) was ignorant of his
[illegible] possessions. An expensive copy of
[illegible] Théâtre," bound by Trautz-Bau-
[illegible] sold for £300.

[illegible] desirable, yet not hopelessly
[illegible] "Virgil" of 1636. Heinsius was the
[illegible] beautiful volume, prettily printed,
[illegible] Probably it is hard to correct
[illegible] accuracy works in the clear but
[illegible] the Elzevirs affected. They
[illegible] by the elegance of their books,
[illegible] to sell good books cheap,
[illegible] The small type was required
[illegible] into little bulk. Nicholas

C

Heinsius, the son of the editor of [illegible] when he came to correct his fath[illegible] found that it contained so many [illegible] misprints, as to be nearly the most [illegible] copy in the world. Heyne says, [illegible] 'Virgil' be one of the rare Elzevirs [illegible] please, but within it has scarcely a tra[illegible] good quality." Yet the first edition [illegible] beautiful little book, with its two pa[illegible] red letters, is so desirable that, till [illegible] possess it, Charles Nodier would not pro[illegible] shelves by any "Virgil" at all.

Equally fine is the "Cæsar" of 163[illegible] with the "Virgil" of 1636 and the "Imi[illegible] without date, M. Willems thinks the mo[illegible] cessful work of the Elzevirs, "one of th[illegible] enviable jewels in the casket of the biblio[illegible] It may be recognised by the page 149, wh[illegible] erroneously printed 153. A good average [illegible] is from 125 to 128 millimetres. The [illegible] known is 130 millimetres. This, bo[illegible] the "Imitation," has one of the pretty [illegible] genious frontispieces which the Elze[illegible] fixed to their books. So farewell, [illegible] speed in your sport, ye hunters of El[illegible] may you find perhaps the missel [illegible] "L'Aimable Mère de Jésus."

BALLADE OF THE REAL AND IDEAL.

(DOUBLE REFRAIN.)

O VISIONS of salmon tremendous,
Of trout of unusual weight,
Of waters that wander as Ken does,
Ye come through the Ivory Gate!
But the skies that bring never a "spate,"
But the flies that catch up in a thorn,
But the creel that is barren of freight,
Through the portals of horn!

O dreams of the Fates that attend us
With prints in the earliest state,
O bargains in books that they send us,
Ye come through the Ivory Gate!
But the tome that has never a mate,
But the quarto that's tattered and torn,
And bereft of a title and date,
Through the portals of horn!

O dreams of the tongues that commend us,
Of crowns for the laureate pate,
Of a public to buy and befriend us,
Ye come through the Ivory Gate!
But the critics that slash us and slate,[1]
But the people that hold us in scorn,
But the sorrow, the scathe, and the hate,
Through the portals of horn!

ENVOY.

Fair dreams of things golden and great,
Ye come through the Ivory Gate;
But the facts that are bleak and forlorn,
Through the portals of horn!

[1] "Slate" is a professional term for a severe criticism. Clearly the word is originally "slat," a narrow board of wood, with which a person might be beaten.

This was the note in earlier editions, but, in the *Athenæum*, October 31, 1891, Mr. Skeat gives another derivation, and insists that from his verdict only dull and ignorant people can differ. Οὐ φροντὶς Ἱπποκλείδῃ.

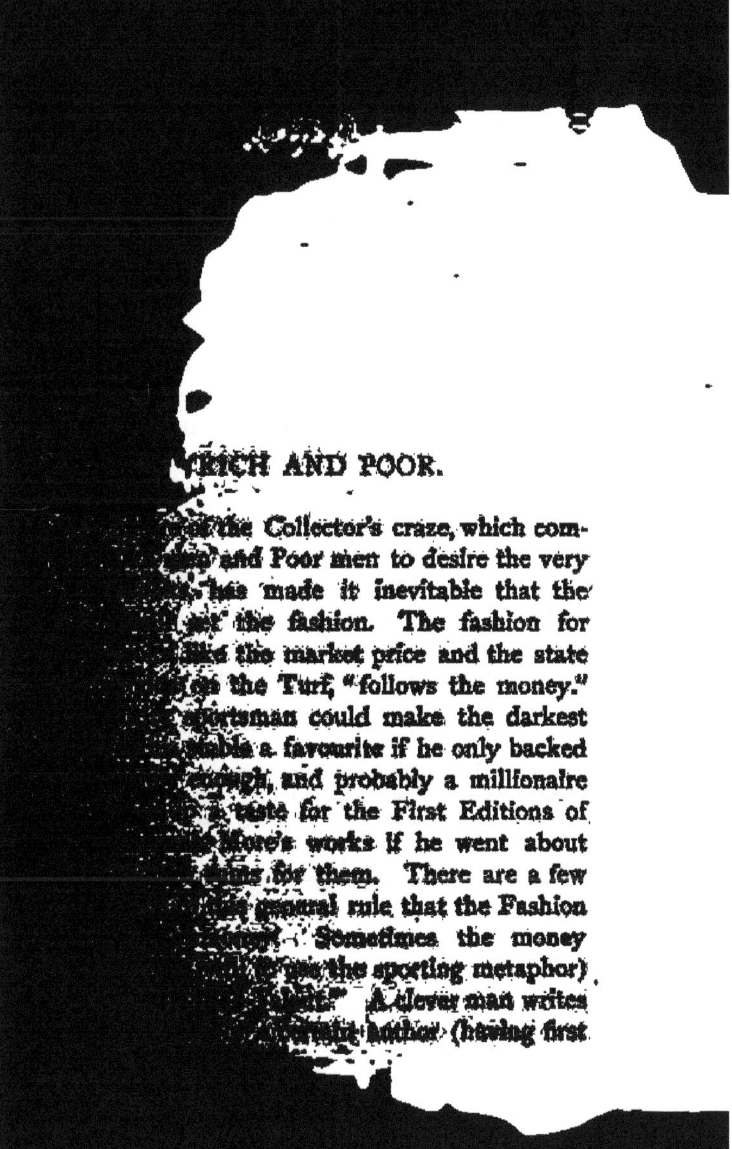

RICH AND POOR.

of the Collector's craze, which com- and Poor men to desire the very has made it inevitable that the set the fashion. The fashion for like the market price and the state on the Turf, "follows the money." sportsman could make the darkest a favourite if he only backed enough, and probably a millionaire a taste for the First Editions of More's works if he went about for them. There are a few general rule that the Fashion Sometimes the money to use the sporting metaphor) A clever man writes author (having first carefully provided himself with that [illegible] works), and then the rich collector [illegible] head and invests heavily, perhaps, in [illegible] la Bretonne. Nodier sometimes made [illegible] of this kind, but Nodier was often [illegible] age. He possessed a beautiful example of [illegible] rault's "Contes de ma Mère l'Oye" [illegible] 1697), and he tried to write it into [illegible] But in Nodier's time it did not sell for [illegible] than six or seven pounds. The price of [illegible] pleasant fountain-head of fairy tales is [illegible] literally, beyond rubies. In recent [illegible] of M. Damascène Morgand and of M. [illegible] one finds no example of Perrault's first [illegible] editions. Both merchants offer the [illegible] print at prices varying from £60 to £80.[1] [illegible] says, but perhaps too hastily, that the [illegible]

[1] "Perrault, *Histoires ou contes du temps passé*, [illegible] *moralités*. Par le fils de Monsieur Perrault, de l'[illegible] françoise. *Suivant la copie, à Paris* (Amsterdam. [illegible] Pet. in 12. front grav. et fig. mar. fil. dos orné, [illegible] (TRAUTZ BAUZONNET.)" Apparently the [illegible] *Académie Francois.* It is curious to see how [illegible] sistently survive in these old popular works. The [illegible] of *Contes de ma Mère l'Oye*, the group of the old [illegible] ning and telling her tale by the cottage fire to the [illegible] the cat, is only slightly modified in "[illegible] Edition of Mother Goose. (Glasgow, [illegible] (*sic*) with Elegant Engravings." It is all [illegible] the Dutch reprint to the Elzevirs, but M. [illegible] it in his great work.

[illegible] in the original Paris edition. I [illegible] one copy of the latter, in the [illegible] of a London Bookseller. [illegible] not succeed in making it fashionable [illegible] day; he was less fortunate than [illegible] found a quantity of uncut Eliza[illegible] in Hungary, and then wrote on [illegible] they became a treasure. But Time [illegible] round his revenges, and Nodier is [illegible] Only the rich can buy the original [illegible] de ma Mère l'Oye" of 1697. [illegible] poor man may light on it in [illegible] Box, that Fortunatus's cap [illegible] that casket of Pandora, which [illegible] Hope at the bottom of its dusty [illegible] pretty modern fairy tale might be [illegible] the King with three sons who sent [illegible] adventure, to find Perrault's first

[illegible] not have a better text than this [illegible] a sermon about the Books of the [illegible] and the Books of the Poor Man. [illegible] that both desire, and, as virtue [illegible] in *pauperum taberna*, the Poor [illegible] reason for his choice. He [illegible] love of Perrault himself, for [illegible] tales that come to us so [illegible] nurse's story lisped out in

courtly language by Perrault's little...
signs himself

de Votre Altesse Royale
Le très humble et très obeissant serviteur,
P. D'ARMANCOUR,

in his dedication to MADEMOISELLE.

But the wicked Rich Man merely desires... tiny tome because it is rare and precious,... has no thought of editing Perrault's "Contes"... And it is an example of the touching fashion... which the Poor Man gleans in the Rich Man's harvest field, that *he* readily welcomes... cherishes quite a late copy of Mother Goose... This little shabby cropped copy in sheep... has, at least, the ancient spelling, the old frontis-piece, the tiny rude vignettes on copper... were the children's books of our great-great-grandfathers; here you see the king in... with eagles' heads on the bedposts; here a... as big as the wolf Fenris of the Twilight of the Gods is about to swallow Red Riding Hood's grandmother at one gulp. Here is Puss in Boots, as tall as his Master, the Marquis... little Hop o' my Thumb, in a frock...

¹ "*Histoires ou Contes du Tems passé*..." Par Mr. Perrault. Nouvelle Edition augmentée... à la fin. A Amsterdam, Chez Jaques Desbordes... Porte de la Bourse. M.DCC.XXIX... black and red.

[illegible] books from the shop-
[illegible] respectable-looking person;
[illegible] is climbing from the tower to
[illegible] cluster up in cocked hats even
[illegible] brandishing his cruel sabre. This is
[illegible] Rock of fairy Bibliography, but it
[illegible] the Blue Rose, and retains some-
[illegible] morocco fragrance. Thus the heart
[illegible] Man is glad, in the reflected joy of
[illegible] lasses who thumbed Mother
[illegible] French nurseries long ago. But the
[illegible] would throw the *bouquin* into the
[illegible] basket.

[illegible] original Perrault, the relic, the
[illegible] of Folk Lore is lost, like the grave
[illegible] the Rich Man has invented sub-
[illegible] Perrault of 1742 and the Perrault
[illegible] These and the reflections they suggest
[illegible] to the last and fiercest fancy of the
[illegible], the fancy for the illustrated
[illegible] of 1750-1800. Here he is in an
[illegible] garden of Bibliomania, where we
[illegible] him who have not the golden
[illegible] golden land."

[illegible] catalogues of the famous collec-
[illegible] *Bibliophile*, the delight of
[illegible] and lately purchased by
[illegible] and M. Beraldi's

description of the Perrault of 1742 [illegible] let's copy of "Contes du Temps [illegible] inserted the tales of Griselidis, Peau [illegible] Les Souhaits Ridicules from the edition [illegible] M. Beraldi adds, "In Book collecting [illegible] impenetrable mysteries." Yes, in the [illegible] collections of luxurious opulence! "The [illegible] of 1742 is the *Right* edition, with the [illegible] the freshest state. Yet it rules low [illegible] *bas prix*).[2] On the other hand, the [illegible] 1781 costs from £120 to £160. Why? [illegible] it is an unparalleled example of stinginess [illegible] the publisher Lamy. First, this economi[illegible] the plates of 1742. But he needed fro[illegible] pieces for the additional stories. He ha[illegible] two engraved, and used both of them twi[illegible] That is why the edition of 1781 is such [illegible] markable book." This is, indeed, a [illegible] The Rich Man pays £10 for a book [illegible] the plates are fresh, and £160 for a [illegible] which they are not so fresh, becau[illegible] Publisher was so stingy![3]

[1] Par Perrault (Coustelier), in 12mo, figures de [illegible]

[2] From 200 to 250 francs. Cohen.

[3] Nothing is more instructive, as to changes [illegible] copy of an early edition of Brunet, say of 1820, [illegible] that the original and the first Dutch edition [illegible] mentioned at all. These had no [illegible] illustrated edition of 1781 is mentioned [illegible]

[illegible] most likely to follow the Rich [illegible] which perhaps justify the book- [illegible]. Indeed he cannot follow [illegible] in collecting the famed French [illegible] books. For this there is an excellent [illegible] these works, copiously adorned with [illegible] (and indelicate) engravings on copper, [illegible] prized when they are in the very prime [illegible]. They must be on the largest or [illegible] used when they were first sub- [illegible] by the Parisian amateurs. They [illegible] bound in morocco, by famed binders [illegible] chiefly Derome and Padeloup, and [illegible] must be bright and untarnished. [illegible] London bookseller had a copy of the [illegible] of La Fontaine, the noted edition of [illegible] which Eisen designed vignettes [illegible] in spite of the absurd badness of the [illegible] many cases), and for which Choffard [illegible] exquisite tail-pieces. This copy [illegible] old blue morocco, and the fly-leaf [illegible] ticket of Derome, which, for some [illegible], is rarely found. The back is

[illegible] engravings, it sold for 40 francs. A copy [illegible] the original drawings, actually fetched £27. [illegible] Perhaps in the collection of the Duc [illegible] M. Portalis says, that the book [illegible] Perhaps it is in England still. *Du-* [illegible]

tooled with a decorative pattern ...
lyres, said to have been drawn ...
There is a luxurious rose-coloured ...
ing, or *doublure*, and the book was ...
presentation copy, a type of the ...
pretty Madame du Barry's time. ...
relic of gay pre-Revolutionary France ...
suffered, as Turner's water colours ...
the light of day. The famous "Derome ...
does not seem to stand the sunlight ...
to a yellowish green in some cases, ...
book is kept in a drawer. This is pres...
the reason why the Rich Man greatly ...
the old French books in *red* morocco ...
period, which tarnishes less than the ...
blues. Still, tarnished, or faded, or ...
"Contes" of 1762 are beyond the reach ...
Poor Man. He will not find them on any ...
which, perhaps, is all the better for his ...

In the matter of these illustrated books ...
Rich Man has sought out many devices ...
books are made the victims of what a ...
bookseller calls "The Higher Faking" ...
"fake" is to alter artificially, to ...
triciously: it is hard to find any ...
for the cosmetics of the book ...
a book was originally published ...
but one set of engravings ...

[illegible] collector would take a [illegible] and inept examples of the [illegible] stage, even when they were [illegible] styled *eaux-fortes*—merely [illegible] had completed his set, the [illegible] contemporary buyer had it nobly bound [illegible] Trautz; perhaps he was even wise [illegible] in the Original Wrapper. The [illegible] Original Wrappers is now worth [illegible] bank notes. A copy of this kind, in [illegible] is a thing beyond the hopes of men [illegible] born.

[illegible] a copy in wrapper is discovered, [illegible] then it is treated by the Rich [illegible] same luxurious way. But here a [illegible] among amateurs. There is a [illegible] the last century, "Les Chansons [illegible] 1773, 4 vol. in 4, "figures de [illegible]." M. Paillet succeeded in [illegible] uncut. It had belonged [illegible] to Aguillon, Grésy, and [illegible] of these intelligent men had [illegible] charms. One had secured [illegible] of the first volume. [illegible] the collective industry of all, [illegible] the *eaux-fortes*. There are [illegible] of the portrait of [illegible] in an interesting condition.

One of these was obtained with [illegible]
La Borde himself.

When M. Paillet had brought [illegible]
this pitch of perfection, he took a [illegible]
tion. *He had it bound!* The [illegible]
passionately canvassed the question [illegible]
Paillet wise? The binding was by [illegible]
morocco, *doublé* with blue, tooled in [illegible]
the decorative designs on the panels [illegible]
Trianon. What of that? The fresh[illegible]
departed, the virginal charm of the [illegible]
can never be restored. Moreover, one [illegible]
the medallion of Marie Antoinette, is [illegible]
And some one else bought that rarest [illegible]
engravings for six francs. This is what [illegible]
of "faking." Better were it to leave [illegible]
alone. But "the *lower* faking," the [illegible]
and altering of books, is commonly a [illegible]
not a very worthy trick.[1]

[1] Confession is good for man: let me confess [illegible]
"faked" a book myself. It was an instance of [illegible]
follies of the Poor Man. It befell me once to [illegible]
shilling "Moral Maxims and Reflections, writ[illegible]
the Duke of Rochefoucault. Now made [illegible]
Printed for M. Gillyflower in Westminster Hall, [illegible]
is the first English Rochefoucauld. "[illegible]
attempted part of it," says the translator, [illegible]
have intended a perfect work, so much [illegible]
and her *Lysander*, with such [illegible]
as her Darling Passion of [illegible]

[illegible] Bonic," which M. Paillet [illegible] bound, was, in human memory, [illegible] Paul Lacroix says that, in his [illegible] mouldered on the *quais* in [illegible] bought the "Chansons," in [illegible] for £2 10s., and gave them to [illegible] who handed them over to her [illegible] upon. The old editions of [illegible] the book at about forty francs. [illegible] sellers ask about £160. Of all [illegible] been, posthumously, the luckiest. [illegible] Baron Roger Portalis) in 1734, [illegible] Mousquetaires, where he was a [illegible], a kind of Aramis. He left [illegible] a pious aunt, and took to [illegible] not pious. He ruined himself [illegible] prodigal taste for beautiful en- [illegible] books hastened his doom. Debts [illegible] killed him in 1780. He made a [illegible] before his death, and expired, [illegible] freshly powdered, in his chair. [illegible] were once in every Poor Man's [illegible] Men had not set the fashion, [illegible] follow it. In 1821 the "Fables

[illegible] "Maxims" (Paris, 1665), a copy [illegible], still having no frontispiece. I had [illegible], so that I don't know which it is [illegible] English frontispiece into the French

Nouvelles," on Large Paper, ... the designs, sold for a louis ... (Paris, 1770), *with the original designs* ... nineteen francs! But now it is, ... "the thirteenth labour of Hercules" ... the complete engravings, in good ... and with the *eaux-fortes*. This passion ... men to excesses, like the old Dutch ... tulips.

Foolish or not, the fashion, and his ... it, has gained Dorat a shadow of immortality. The epigram on him, untranslatable as ... on a pun, is justified.

> Lorsque j'admire ces estampes,
> Ces vignettes, ces culs de lampe,
> Je crois voir en toi, pauvre auteur,
> Pardonne à mon humeur trop franche,
> Un malheureux navigateur
> Qui se sauve de planche en planche.

A good illustration of the Rich Man's ... M. Paillet's adventure with Fragonard's ... designs for La Fontaine's "Contes" ... Paris, 1795). M. Paillet acquired, ... a beautifully written copy of La ... "Contes;" nay, he actually made ... acquiring it. *Habent sua fata* ... beautiful quartos, bound in ... Derome and copied out by ...

[illegible] fifty-seven original
[illegible] work was written
[illegible] the Fermiers Généraux,
[illegible] drawings. When
[illegible] these volumes, they were
[illegible] This does not seem dear;
[illegible] thought it was a good deal to
[illegible] to give, that is, in solid cash,
[illegible] write a cheque for £1000.
[illegible] another way, by the ancient
[illegible] barter. He sacrificed to
[illegible] bookseller, a "Faublas," with
[illegible] by Marillier and the suave
[illegible] with orange) by Trautz.
[illegible] Perrault (1781) were also
[illegible] M. Paillet was more readily
[illegible] for the departure of his
[illegible] edition). The Heptameron
[illegible] original comedies of Regnard,
[illegible] of Restif (*vile damnum*)
[illegible] way, and £120 in actual
[illegible] *Tantæ molis erat*—at
[illegible] won his manuscript
[illegible] not at all the kind of
[illegible] would have sent to
[illegible] of a Senator of
[illegible] half the story. M.
[illegible] drawings by Moreau

and his MSS. for five or
cheque. But how did he
bargain? Why, M. Rouquette
engravings of the designs, and
about £3600, of which M. Paillet
Indeed we may say, *Habenti*
had a poor collector such luck!

Such are the successes of
brilliant books, all so fresh, so fair
raiment; are the results of taste and
well as of money. M. Beraldi
Paillet seated in his library, with
five unbound copies of one volume
comparing, selecting, examining with
scope, page by page. The result is
copy, to be perfectly bound, by Cuzin
and to be *le plus bel exemplaire connu*;

These are not, after all, the enjoy
poor collector envies most. He really
read his books, not that he could
modern reprints, but he likes to see
masterpieces of old as Shakespeare
when his quartos were cried at the
Globe, as "book o' the Play."
collector can never have that pleasure
visits Mr. Locker's library and
of Shakspeare quartos. But
cropped, maimed

[illegible] almost his [illegible] with a page- [illegible] these twopenny trea- [illegible] a trifle apocryphal.*

[illegible] is apt to burden himself [illegible] relics out of pure senti- [illegible]

[illegible] London, 1648) I found in a box [illegible] Street. It had belonged, apparently, [illegible] and certainly to Collet's son, who [illegible] an inscription in a beautiful hand, [illegible] *Lucasta* (1649), by Richard Love- [illegible] perfect, is almost not to be found. The [illegible] Locker's catalogue the Rowfant copy [illegible] facsimile of Frontispiece by Hollar, [illegible] But Mr. Locker has now supplied the [illegible] which he purchased, for a ransom, at the [illegible] "Hollar collectors and other wild men [illegible] and prints out of most of the books of [illegible]

[illegible] Rich or Poor, has a library so rich in [illegible] author of these pages. Two of my [illegible] such concern, that I make bold to lay [illegible] benevolent public. I possess (in green [illegible] copy of *The Angler's Delight*, [illegible] London, 1676. But this copy has [illegible] portion of the same book, namely [illegible] Hackney River, with the Names of [illegible] The only Stands there, now, are [illegible] If any bibliophile has the other [illegible] for the whole; and the same [illegible] to-wit, of *Les Œuvres de* [illegible] These volumes, of which I [illegible] the name *Orientaux* is [illegible] ment. He can scarcely [illegible] harmed example of a rare [illegible] lives in hope of completing his [illegible] pleasing aspirations! The two [illegible] imperfect work, like the two lovers [illegible] were one body and soul, in the [illegible] Aristophanes, wander round the world [illegible] meet again. And I think of these [illegible] volumes pained with a *nostalgia*, like [illegible] two obelisks in Théophile Gautier's [illegible] afflicted with "an intense yearning for [illegible] which the Soul desires and cannot [illegible] which she has only a dark and doubtful [illegible] ment."[1]

The tomes are divided for ever. One [illegible] may be in Paris, one on a stall in [illegible] the monoliths estranged, and no more [illegible] united than these *obélisques dépareillés* [illegible]

It is easy to give the poor collector [illegible] advice, to bid him never waste his [illegible] on imperfections, never spend his [illegible] *bouquins*, but wait, and "lie low" [illegible] would-be purchaser of Mark Twain's [illegible] Mexican plug"), till he has a chance [illegible] a real prize. This was the method [illegible] fabled collector, Le Cousin [illegible] wonderful story of his treasure [illegible]

1 Aristophanes in the [illegible]

[illegible] It is one of
[illegible] Moreover, the Poor
[illegible] and self-denial
[illegible] in brown shabby
[illegible] the Rich Man would not
[illegible] of their contents. They
[illegible] scraps of information, waifs of
[illegible] from the dead Court life of
[illegible] I have mislaid—for they lightly
[illegible] go—a volume of courtly
[illegible] in which an Abbé and a
[illegible] discourse on ghosts with a lady of
[illegible] woman has had "an insolent
[illegible] to death by her valets. She
[illegible] is always seeing his ghost, a
[illegible] which the Abbé and philosopher
[illegible] her, with arguments drawn from
[illegible] Religion. No other punishment
[illegible] Ghost inflicted, has dared to
[illegible] *grande dame de par le monde.*
[illegible] was, when this kind of conversa-
[illegible] possible, but probably was
[illegible] gossip. It was the little black
[illegible] this peep into the age of
[illegible] of Alceste, who might well
[illegible] of pretty Célimène, who
[illegible] acted like the cruel

The Poor Man, if he may [illegible] actually enjoy the books which [illegible] keep idle in gilded saloons. [illegible] is a volume for the student [illegible] Marriage: it is *De veteri ritu* [illegible] *& jure* CONNUBIORUM. [illegible] sonius,

Antonius } Hotmanus.
Franciscus }

Apud Franciscum Hackium [illegible]

LVG. BATAVOR

CIↃIↃCXLI.

You buy it for fourpence, nay, for [illegible] with its frontispiece of Adam flirting [illegible] in Paradise. But, let it be in a moroc[illegible] and the Bookseller shall charge [illegible] pounds, and attribute its binding to [illegible] Surely better is sheepskin, for twopen[illegible] content therewith, than, for £15, Pa[illegible] without his ticket!

So we might illustrate the joys of the [illegible] collector. But Charles Lamb has [illegible] things immortal in his prose, and Th[illegible] his verse.

This snug little chamber is crammed in all [illegible]
With worthless old knicknacks, and silly [illegible]
And foolish old odds and foolish old [illegible]
Crack'd bargains from brokers [illegible]

Old armour, prints, pictures, pipes, china (all crack'd),
Old rickety tables, and chairs broken back'd,
A twopenny treasury, wondrous to see.
What matter? 'Tis pleasant to you, friend, and me.[1]

"All cracked" indeed, the cynic may cry, we and our treasures. But men may have their toys, like children; and the Rich Man boasts his wax doll with moveable eyes, and the Poor Man has his fetish of rags tied up with a string, and is as happy as his opulent neighbour.

The price of the original edition of Perrault's Tales is no longer far above rubies. A copy was sold by auction in Paris (March, 1872) for £85. Still the book is very rare. The public libraries of Paris possess but one example.

[1] *Ballads*, by W. M. Thackeray. London: Bradbury and Evans, Bouverie Street. 1856. In the Original Wrapper!

DORIS'S BOOKS.

Doris, on your shelves I note
  Many a grave ancestral tome.
These, perhaps, you have by rote;
  These are constantly at home.
    Ah, but many a gap I spy
    Where Miss Broughton's novels lie!

Doris, there, behind the glass,
  On your Sheratonian shelves—
Oft I see them as I pass—
  Stubbs and Freeman sun themselves.
    All unread I watch them stand;
    That's *Belinda* in your hand!

Doris, I, as you may know,
  Am myself a Man of Letters,
But my learnèd volumes go
  To the top shelf, like my betters,
    High—so high that Doris could
    Scarce get at them if she would!

Doris, there be books of mine,
  That I gave you, wrote your name in,
Tooled and gilded, fair and fine:
  Don't you ever peep the same in?
    Yes, I see you've kept them—but,
    Doris, they are "Quite Uncut!"

Quite uncut, "unopened" rather
  Are mine edifying pages,
From this circumstance I gather
  That some other Muse engages,
    Doris, your misguided fancy:
    Yes, I thought so—reading *Nancy.*

Well, when you are *older*, Doris,
  Wiser, too, you'll love my verses;
Celia likes them, and, what more is,
  Oft—to me—their praise rehearses.
    "*Celia's Thirty,*" did I hear?
    Doris, too, can be severe!

THE ROWFANT BOOKS.

BALLADE EN GUISE DE RONDEAU.

THE Rowfant books, how fair they shew,
The Quarto quaint, the Aldine tall,
Print, autograph, portfolio!
Back from the outer air they call,
The athletes from the Tennis ball,
This Rhymer from his rod and hooks,
Would I could sing them one and all,
The Rowfant books!

The Rowfant books! In sun and snow
They're dear, but most when tempests fall;
The folio towers above the row
As once, o'er minor prophets,—Saul!
What jolly jest books and what small
"Dear dumpy Twelves" to fill the nooks.
You do not find on every stall
The Rowfant books!

The Rowfant books! These long ago
  Were chained within some College hall;
These manuscripts retain the glow
  Of many a coloured capital;
While yet the Satires keep their gall,
  While the Pastissier puzzles cooks,
Theirs is a joy that does not pall,
    The Rowfant books!

ENVOI.

The Rowfant books,—ah magical
  As famed Armida's "golden looks,"
They hold the rhymer for their thrall,
    The Rowfant books.

TO F. L.

I MIND that Forest Shepherd's saw,
  For, when men preached of Heaven, quoth he,
" It's a' that's bricht, and a' that's braw,
  But Bourhope's guid eneuch for me ! "

Beneath the green deep-bosomed hills
  That guard Saint Mary's Loch it lies,
The silence of the pastures fills
  That shepherd's homely paradise.

Enough for him his mountain lake,
  His glen the burn went singing through,
And Rowfant, when the thrushes wake,
  May well seem good enough for you.

For all is old, and tried, and dear,
  And all is fair, and round about
The brook that murmurs from the mere
  Is dimpled with the rising trout.

But when the skies of shorter days
  Are dark and all the ways are mire,
How bright upon your books the blaze
  Gleams from the cheerful study fire.

On quartos where our fathers read,
  Enthralled, the book of Shakespeare's play,
On all that Poe could dream of dread,
  And all that Herrick sang of gay!

Fair first editions, duly prized,
  Above them all, methinks, I rate
The tome where Walton's hand revised
  His wonderful receipts for bait!

Happy, who rich in toys like these
  Forgets a weary nation's ills,
Who from his study window sees
  The circle of the Sussex hills!

SOME JAPANESE BOGIE-BOOKS.

THERE is, or used to be, a poem for infant minds of a rather Pharisaical character, which was popular in the nursery when I was a youngster. It ran something like this :—

> I thank my stars that I was born
> A little British child.

Perhaps these were not the very words, but that was decidedly the sentiment. Look at the Japanese infants, from the pencil of the famous Hokusai. Though they are not British, were there ever two jollier, happier small creatures? Did Leech, or Mr. Du Maurier, or Andrea della Robbia ever present a more delightful view of innocent, well-pleased childhood? Well, these Japanese children, if they are in the least inclined to be timid or nervous, must have an awful time of it at night in the dark, and when they make that eerie " northwest passage " bed-

Japanese Children. Drawn by Hokusai.

wards through the darkling house ...
Stevenson sings the perils and ...
All of us who did not suffer ...
brought up on the views of Mr. ...
have endured, in childhood, a good ...
ghosts. But it is nothing to what ...
children bear; for our ghosts are to the ...
of Japan as moonlight is to sunlight ...
water unto whisky. Personally, I ...
that few people have been plagued by ...
that walketh in darkness more than ...
At the early age of ten I had the ...
ingenious Mr. Edgar Poe and of ...
Brontë "put into my hands" by a ...
had served as a Bashi Bazouk, and knew ...
meaning of fear. But I *did*, and ...
Nelson would have found out "what ...
or the boy in the German tale ...
"learned to shiver," if he had been ...
to peruse "Jane Eyre," and the " ...
and the "Fall of the House of ...
was. Every night I expected to wake ...
coffin, having been prematurely ...
hear sighs in the area, followed ...
steady footsteps on the stairs, ...
a lady all in a white shroud, ...
and clay, stagger into my ...
too rapid interment. As to the ...

[illegible]
[illegible]
[illegible]
[illegible] a harm-
[illegible] disturbing,
[illegible] Yellow Dwarf," who
[illegible] of the Countess
[illegible] infant into
[illegible] a time of it in
[illegible] happy British child
[illegible] are nothing to the
[illegible] only night but day
[illegible] infants of Japan and
[illegible]

[illegible] probably much the same
[illegible] Japanese have borrowed
[illegible] and awesome
[illegible] from the Chinese, and
[illegible] the original model,
[illegible] complete, and horror-
[illegible] Chinese *haunts* (as the
[illegible] call them) from
[illegible] translated scores of
[illegible] his "Strange Tales
[illegible] (De la Rue, 1880). Mr.
[illegible] China is the place
[illegible] of the Psychical

Ghosts do not live [illegible]
China, but boldly come out [illegible]
in the pleasures and business [illegible]
always been a question with [illegible]
in a haunted house, appear [illegible]
audience. What does the [illegible]
tried chamber do when the [illegible]
no guest is put in the room [illegible]
the haunted room? Does the [illegible]
complain that there is "no house [illegible]
to rehearse his little performance [illegible]
scientious and disinterestedly artistic [illegible]
deprived of the artist's true pleasure [illegible]
ing of sympathetic emotion in the [illegible]
spectator? We give too little [illegible]
sympathy to ghosts, who in our [illegible]
country houses often find no [illegible]
from year's end to year's end [illegible]
then is a guest placed in the " [illegible]
Then I like to fancy the glee [illegible]
green, or the radiant boy, or the [illegible]
or the old gentleman in snuff [illegible]
as he, or she, recognises the [illegible]
spectator, and prepares to give [illegible]
effects in the familiar style. [illegible]

Now in China and Japan [illegible]
does not wait till people [illegible]
room; a ghost, like a person [illegible]

A STORM-FIEND.

everywhere." [illegible] excellence, that very [illegible] from an embodied [illegible] mortality so cleverly that [illegible] been known to personate [illegible] honours, and pass an examina[illegible] pleasing example of this kind [illegible] limitations of ghosts, is told in [illegible] A gentleman of Huai Shang, [illegible] had arrived at the age of fifty, [illegible] consisted of but one son, a fine boy, [illegible] averse from study," as if there [illegible] strange in *that*. One day the son [illegible] mysteriously, as people do from [illegible] a year he came back, said he had [illegible] in a Taoist monastery, and, to all [illegible] ment, took to his books. Next year [illegible] his B.A. degree, a First Class. All [illegible] bourhood was overjoyed, for Huai [illegible] like Pembroke College (Oxford), [illegible] ing to the poet, "First Class [illegible] far between." It was who [illegible] honour of giving his daughter [illegible] intellectual marvel. A very [illegible] selected, but most unexpectedly [illegible] not marry. This nearly broke [illegible] The old gentleman knew, [illegible] belief, that if he had no gra[illegible]

generation to feed his
will the little needful
then, the father naming
day;" till K'o-ch'ang, B.A.,
His mother tried to
his clothes "came off in her
vanished! Next day
flesh-and-blood son, who had
and enslaved. The genuine
overjoyed to hear of his ap-
The rites were duly cele-
than a year the old gentle-
his much-longed-for grandchild.
K'o-ch'ang, though very jolly
beloved, was as stupid as ever,
but the sporting intelligence
It was now universally
the learned K'o-ch'ang had been
clever ghost. It follows that
a very good degree; but ladies
of marrying ghosts, owing to
of these learned spectres.
is by no means always a
as, indeed, has already been
the affecting narrative of the
examination. Even the
in China to the statue in
which accepts invita-

tions to dinner, is anything
guest. So much may be gathered
story of Chu and Lu. Chu was
graduate of great courage and
but dull of wit. He was a married
his children (as in the old Oxford
often rushed into their mother's presence
ing, "Mamma! mamma! papa's been
again!" Once it chanced that Chu
wine party, and the negus (a favourite
of the Celestials) had done its work
young friends betted Chu a bird's-nest
that he would not go to the nearest
enter the room devoted to coloured
representing the torments of Purgatory
carry off the image of the Chinese judge
dead, their Osiris or Rhadamanthus.
old Chu, and soon returned with the
effigy (which wore "a green face, a
and a hideous expression") in his arms
other men were frightened, and begged
restore his worship to his place on the
bench. Before carrying back the
magistrate, Chu poured a libation
and said, "Whenever your excellency
disposed, I shall be glad to take
with you in a friendly way."
as Chu was taking a stirrup

[illegible] came to the
[illegible] put the kettle
[illegible] made a night of it
[illegible] Their friendship was
[illegible] that moment. The
[illegible] a new heart (literally)
[illegible] to pass examinations;
[illegible] is the seat of all the
[illegible] Mrs. Chu, a plain
[illegible] the ghost provided a
[illegible] girl recently slain by
[illegible] Chu's death the genial
[illegible] neglect him, but obtained for
[illegible] as registrar in the next
[illegible] rank attached.

[illegible] among the Chinese, seems
[illegible] bureaucracy, patent places,
[illegible] and tails, and, in short,
[illegible]. All civilised readers
[illegible] Mr. Stockton's humorous
[illegible] Transferred Ghost." In Mr.
[illegible] does not always get his
[illegible] a vigorous competition
[illegible] ghostships, and a great
[illegible] party feeling. It may be
[illegible] spectre gets any
[illegible] then, if he has little
[illegible] to take a chance of

haunting the Board of Trade, o
instead of "walking" in the
One spirit may win a post in
the imperial palace, while an
with a position in an old
perhaps has to follow the
seedy "medium" through
third-rate hotels. Now this is
Chinese view of the fates and fort
Quisque suos patimur manes.

In China, to be brief, and to
(who ought to know what he
about), "supernaturals are to be
where." This is the fact that
puzzling and terrible to a child of
and trustful character. These Ori
do not appear in the dark alone,
haunted houses, or at cross-roads, or
woods. They are everywhere:
his own ghost, every place has its
ing fiend, every natural phenomenon
forming spirit; every quality, as
envy, malice, has an embodied
prowling about seeking what it
Where our science, for example,
smells) sewer gas, the Japanese
meagre, insatiate wrath, crawling
lives of men. Where we

A SNOW BOGIE.

their [illegible]
[illegible]

The illustrations in this pa[illegible] specimens chosen out of [illegible] Japanese bogies. We have [illegible] copy the very most awful specim[illegible] be as horrid as we can. Thes[illegible] ings, too, are generally coloured [illegible] expense, and the colouring is [illegible] horrid and satisfactory. This [illegible] fortunately perhaps, we cannot [illegible] Meanwhile, if any child looks into [illegible] let him (or her) not be alarmed by [illegible] he beholds. Japanese ghosts do not [illegible] country; there are none of them [illegible] Japanese Legation. Just as [illegible] rattlesnakes are not to be seriously [illegible] our woods and commons, so [illegible] ghost cannot breathe (any more [illegible] can) in the air of England or Americ[illegible] not yet even keep any ghostly zoolog[illegible] in which the bogies of Japanese, [illegible] Red Indians, and other distant peop[illegible] accommodated. Such an establish[illegible] haps to be desired in the interests [illegible] research, but that form of research [illegible] been endowed by a enlightened [illegible] government.

The first to attract our attention represents, as I understand, the common ghost, or *simulacrum vulgare* of psychical science. To this complexion must we all come, according to the best Japanese opinion. Each of us contains within him "somewhat of a shadowy being," like the spectre described by Dr. Johnson: something like the Egyptian "Ka," for which the curious may consult the works of Miss Amelia B. Edwards and other learned Orientalists. The most recent French student of these matters, the author of "L'Homme Posthume," is of opinion that we do not all possess this double, with its power of surviving our bodily death. He thinks, too, that our ghost, when it does survive, has but rarely the energy and enterprise to make itself visible to or audible by "shadow-casting men." In some extreme cases the ghost (according to our French authority, that of a disciple of M. Comte) feeds fearsomely on the bodies of the living. In no event does he believe that a ghost lasts much longer than a hundred years. After that it mizzles into spectre, and is resolved into its elements, whatever they may be.

A somewhat similar and (to my own mind) probably sound theory of ghosts prevails among savage tribes, and among such peoples as the

ancient Greeks, the modern
ancestor worshippers. When
all do, or used to do, the ghosts
dead, they gave special attention
of the dead of the last three
ghosts older than the century to
own supplies of meat and drink
gence testifies to a notion that
are of little account, for good or
other hand, as regards the longevity
we must not shut our eyes to the
the bogie in ancient armour which
Glamis Castle, or to the Jesuit
Elizabeth's date that haunts the
very nice place to haunt: I ask no
ghost in the Pavilion at Lord's
scandal) of an English nobleman.
instantiæ contradictoriæ, as Bacon
present to our minds, we must
present condition of psychical
tise too hastily about the span of
the *simulacrum vulgare*. Very
chances of a prolonged existence
ratio to the square of the
which severs him from our
one has ever even pretended
an ancient Roman buried
less of a Pict or Scot

THE SIMULACRUM VULGARE.

welcome as such an
many of us. Thus the
look as if there were a kind of
tions among ghosts, which, from
view, is not an arrangement at
repine.

The Japanese artist expresses
of the casual and fluctuating nature
drawing his spectre in shaky lines
model had given the artist the
simulacrum rises out of the earth
lation, and groups itself into shape
spade with which all that is corporeal
owner has been interred. Please
uncomforted and dismal expression
lacrum. We must remember that
or "Ka" is not the "soul," which
destinies in the future world, good
is only a shadowy resemblance
as in the Egyptian creed, to
tomb and hover near it. The
Japanese have their own
the next world, and we must
confuse the eternal fortunes of
conscious, and responsible
ing other worlds than ours,
vagaries of the semi-material
larva, which so often develop

A WELL AND WATER BOGIE.

fighting disposition quite
its proprietor in life.

The next bogie, so limp and
he seems, with his white, drooping
and hands, reminds us of that
species of apparition, "la lavandière
who washes dead men's linen in
pools and rivers. Whether this
meant for the spirit of the well (for
has its spirit in Japan), or whether
ghost of some mortal drowned in
cannot say with absolute certainty
opinion of the learned tends to the
clusion. Naturally a Japanese child
in the dusk to draw water, will do
and trembling, for this limp, flop
might scare the boldest. Another
terrible creation of fancy, I take to be
about which the curious can
Calmet, who will tell them how
in Hungary have been depopula
pires; or he may study in Fauriel
de la Grèce Moderne" the vamp
Hellas.

Another plan, and perhaps
factory to a timid or superstit
read in a lonely house
named "Carmilla," printed

RAISING THE WIND.

Fanu's "In a Glass Darkly" [illegible]
give you the peculiar sentim[illegible]
will produce a gelid perspiration [illegible]
patient to a condition in which he [illegible]
to look round the room. If, while [illegible]
some one tells him Mr. Augustus H[illegible]
Croglin Grange, his education [illegible]
and theory of vampires will be com[illegible]
will be a very proper and well-qual[illegible]
of Earlswood Asylum. The most [illegible]
vampire, caught red-handed in the ac[illegible]
bestial incarnation of ghoulishne[illegible]
carefully refrained from reproducing [illegible]

Scarcely more agreeable is the [illegible]
blowing from her mouth a malev[illegible]
tion, an embodiment of malignant [illegible]
sorcery. The vapour which flies [illegible]
the mouth constitutes "a sending [illegible]
technical language of Icelandic [illegible]
capable (in Iceland, at all even[illegible]
the form of some detestable super[illegible]
to destroy the life of a hated rival [illegible]
of our last example it is very [illegible]
make head or tail of the spectre [illegible]
Chinks and crannies are his [illegible]
these he drops upon you. [illegible]
not an attractive or genial gh[illegible]
are such "visions about" [illegible]

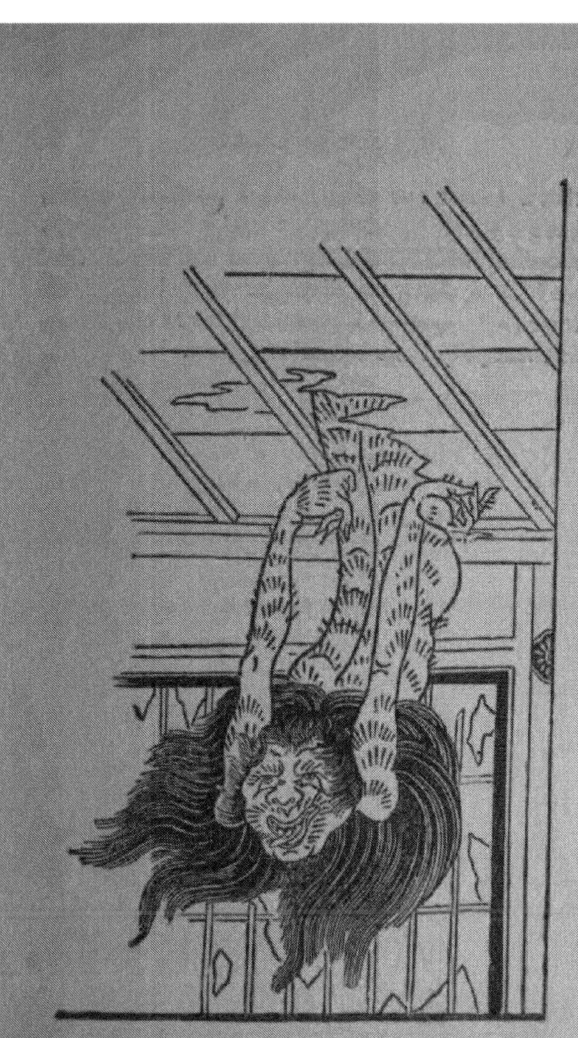

A CHINK AND CREVICE BOGIE.

that children, apt to believe in all such fancies, have a youth of variegated and intense misery, recurring with special vigour at bed-time. But we look again at our first picture, and hope and trust that Japanese boys and girls are as happy as these jolly little creatures appear.

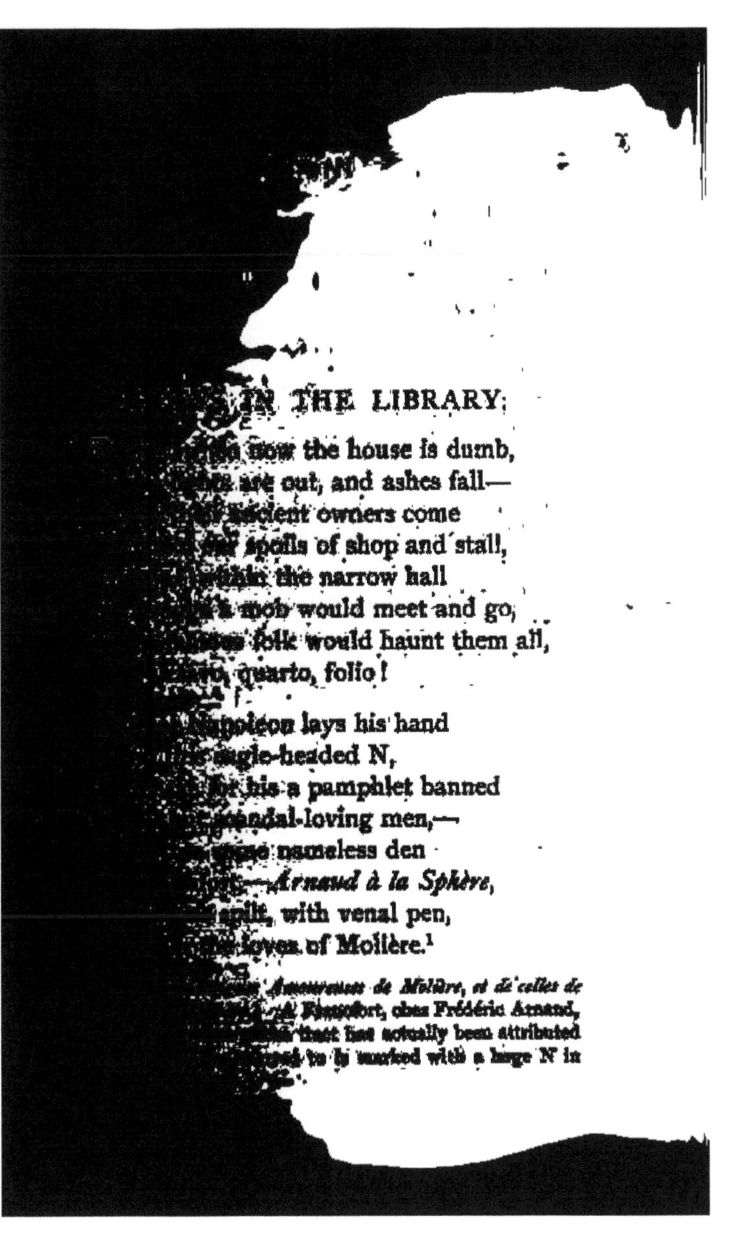

IN THE LIBRARY.

now the house is dumb,
are out, and ashes fall—
ancient owners come
spoils of shop and stall,
the narrow hall
mob would meet and go,
folk would haunt them all,
quarto, folio!

Napoleon lays his hand
eagle-headed N,
his a pamphlet banned
scandal-loving men,—
nameless den
—*Arnaud à la Sphère*,
spilt, with venal pen,
loves of Molière.[1]

Amoureuses de Molière, et de celles de Francfort, chez Frédéric Arnaud, that has actually been attributed to is marked with a large N in

Another shade—he [illegible]
  "Boney," the foeman [illegible]
The great Sir Walter, [illegible]
  With that grave homely [illegible]
He claims his poem of the [illegible]
  That rang Benvoirlich's [illegible]
And *this*, that doth the lineage [illegible]
  And fortunes of the bold [illegible]

. . . . . .

For these were his, and those [illegible]
  To one who dwelt beside the [illegible]
That murmurs with its tiny [illegible]
  To join the Tweed at Ashestiel [illegible]
Now thick as motes the shadows [illegible]
  And find their own, and claim [illegible]
Of books wherein Ribou did deal, [illegible]
  Or Roulland sold to wise Colbert [illegible]

What famous folk of old are here [illegible]
  A royal duke comes down [illegible]
And greatly wants his Elzevir, [illegible]
  His Pagan tutor, Lucius.[3]

[1] *The Lady of the Lake*, 1810.
The Lay of the Last Minstrel, 1806.
"To Mrs. Robert Laidlaw, Peel, [illegible]

[2] *Dictys Cretensis*, Apud Lamb[illegible]
Paris, 1680. In red morocco, with [illegible]

[3] *L. Annæi Senecæ Opera Omnia*, [illegible]
1649. With book-plate of the Duke [illegible]

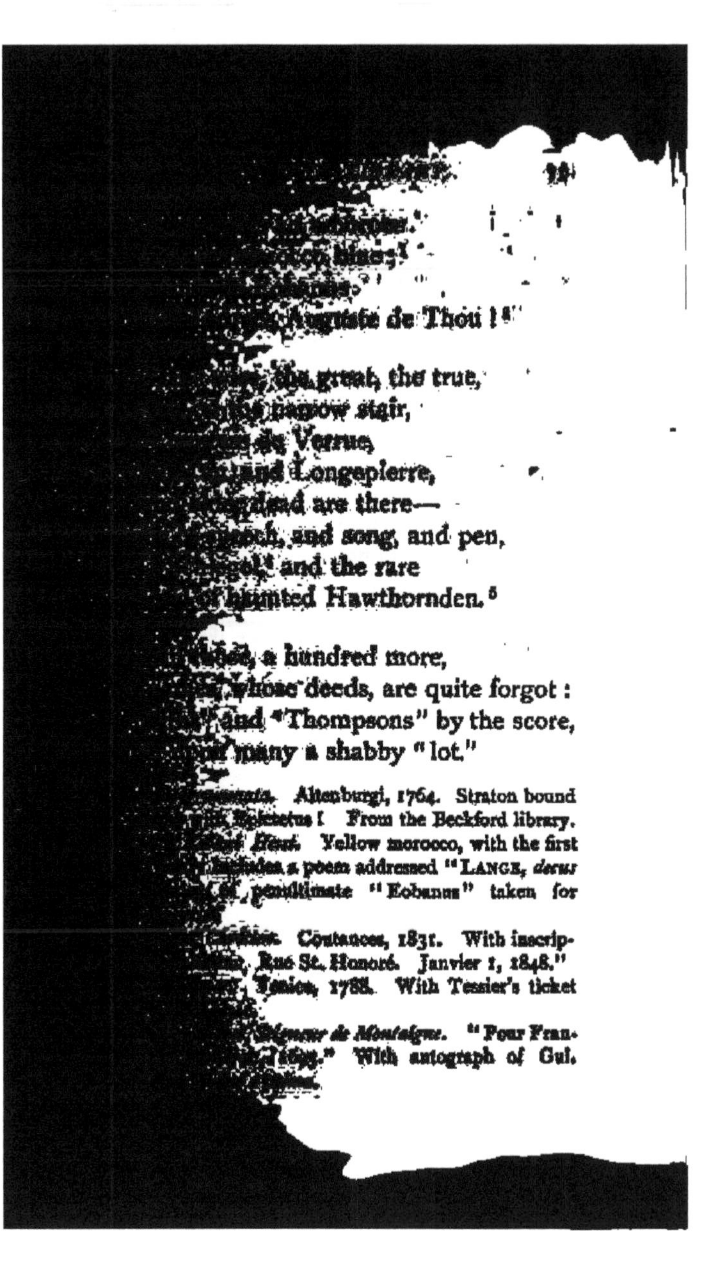

Auguste de Thou ![4]

the great, the true,
narrow stair,
de Verrue,
and Longepierre,
are there—
speech, and song, and pen,
and the rare
of haunted Hawthornden.[5]

a hundred more,
whose deeds, are quite forgot :
and "Thompsons" by the score,
many a shabby "lot."

Altenburgi, 1764. Straton bound Epictetus ! From the Beckford library.
Yellow morocco, with the first includes a poem addressed "LANGE, *decus* penultimate "Eobanus" taken for

Coutances, 1831. With inscrip- Rue St. Honoré. Janvier 1, 1848."
Venice, 1788. With Tessier's ticket

Seigneur de Montaigne. "Pour Fran- 1609." With autograph of Gul.

This playbook was the joy of Pott[1]—
  Pott, for whom now no mortal grieves.
Our names, like his, remembered not,
  Like his, shall flutter on fly-leaves!

At least in pleasant company
  We bookish ghosts, perchance, may flit;
A man may turn a page, and sigh,
  Seeing one's name, to think of it.
Beauty, or Poet, Sage, or Wit,
  May ope our book, and muse awhile,
And fall into a dreaming fit,
  As now we dream, and wake, and smile!

[1] "The little old foxed Molière," once the property of William Pott, unknown to fame.

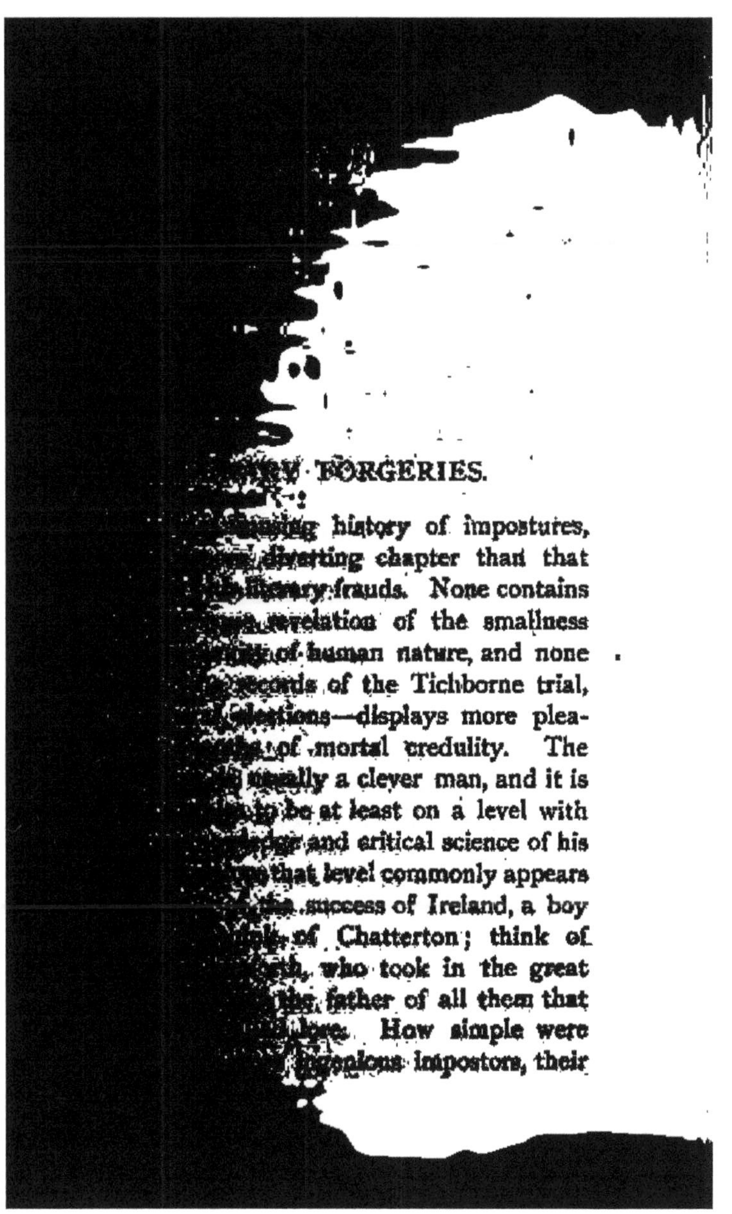

...RY FORGERIES.

history of impostures,
diverting chapter than that
literary frauds. None contains
revelation of the smallness
of human nature, and none
records of the Tichborne trial,
elections—displays more plea-
of mortal credulity. The
usually a clever man, and it is
to be at least on a level with
and critical science of his
that level commonly appears
success of Ireland, a boy
of Chatterton; think of
who took in the great
father of all them that
How simple were
ingenious impostors, their

resources how scanty; how
improvised was their whole
have altered a little. Jo Smith's
famed "Golden Bible" only carried
polygamous *populus qui vult decipi*
little lower than even the believers
Israel. The Moabite Ireland, who
Mr. Shapira the famous MS. of
but did not delude M. Clermont-
doubtless a smart man; he was,
little too indolent, a little too
He might have procured better and
nisable materials than his old
rolls;" in short, he took rather too
and came to the wrong market.
forgery ought first, perhaps, to
credulous, and only slowly should it
the prestige of having already
believers, before the learned world.
scriber of the Phœnician inscription
(of all places) was a clever man,
of the voyage of Hiram to
probably gained some credence
in England it only carried
author of "The Prehistoric
Steel." But the Brazilians,
have dropped the subject,
inscriptions of Brazil are

[illegible] about which one
[illegible] doubts.

[illegible] forger are curiously
[illegible] perhaps, be analysed
[illegible] "push," and love of
[illegible] forgeries have been pious
[illegible] interests of a church,
[illegible] Then we have frauds
[illegible] example, a forger should offer
[illegible] of money to the British
[illegible] he tries to palm off his
[illegible] the "Bad Samaritan" of
[illegible] we come to playful frauds,
[illegible] origin playful, like (perhaps)
[illegible] forgeries of Ireland, the *super-*
[illegible] Mérimée, the sham antique
[illegible] poems in their way) of
[illegible] other examples. Occasionally
[illegible] that forgeries, begun for the
[illegible] the imitative faculty, and
[illegible] against the learned, have been
[illegible] earnest. The humorous deceits
[illegible] pardonable, though it is
[illegible] the young archæologist who
[illegible] with false Greek inscrip-
[illegible] may be a mere fable
[illegible] who are constantly ac-
[illegible] of crimes. Then

there are forgeries by "pushing"
to get a reading for poems which,
new, would be neglected. There rema
of which the motives are so comp
remain for ever obscure. We may
ascribe them to love of notoriety in
such notoriety as Macpherson
dubious pinchbeck Ossian. More diffi
to understand are the forgeries,
scholars have committed or connived at
purpose of supporting some opinion
held with earnestness. There is a vein
ness and self-deceit in the character of
who half-persuades himself that his
facts are true. The Payne Collier
thus one of the most difficult in the
explain, for it is equally hard to supp
Mr. Payne Collier was taken in by
on the folio he gave the world, and
that he was himself guilty of forgery
his own opinions.

The further we go back in the
literary forgeries, the more (as is natu
find them to be of a pious or priestly
When the clergy alone can write,
can forge. In such ages people
chiefly in prophecies and
are careful about literature

[illegible] of title-deeds [illegible] forged a line in the [illegible] ships for the purpose [illegible] belonged to Athens, [illegible] forger, the Ionian father [illegible] Onomacritus. There [illegible] Egyptian inscription pro- [illegible] the fourth, but probably of the [illegible]. The Germans hold the [illegible] French, from patriotic motives, [illegible] opinion. But this forgery [illegible]

[illegible] of Onomacritus without a [illegible] he began the forging business [illegible] was (apart from this failing) [illegible] and magnificently respectable [illegible] scene of the error and the [illegible] Onomacritus presents itself always [illegible] pictorial vision. It is night, [illegible] night of Athens; not of the [illegible] remain, but of the ancient [illegible] ashes during the invasion of [illegible] is the time of Pisistratus the [illegible] the scene is the ancient temple, [illegible] Athene, the fane where the [illegible] on cakes, and the primeval [illegible] the well of Posidon. The [illegible] inmost shrine is lit by the ray of one earthen lamp, [illegible] cern the majestic form of [illegible] stooping above a coffer of [illegible] carved with the exploits of [illegible] with *boustrophedon* inscriptions. [illegible] archaic Athenian wears the badge [illegible] grasshopper. He is Onomacritus, [illegible] poet, and the trusted guardian of [illegible] oracles of Musaeus and Bacis.

What is he doing? Why, he takes [illegible] fragrant cedar coffer certain thin [illegible] of lead, whereon are scratched the [illegible] doom, the prophecies of the Greek [illegible] Rhymer. From his bosom he draws [illegible] thin sheet of lead, also stained and [illegible] On this he scratches, in imitation [illegible] "Cadmeian letters," a prophecy that [illegible] near Lemnos shall disappear under [illegible] So busy is he in this task, that he does [illegible] the rustle of a chiton behind, and [illegible] man's hand is on his shoulder! [illegible] turns in horror. Has the god [illegible] him for tampering with the [illegible] it is Lasus, of Hermione, a [illegible] has caught the keeper of the [illegible] very act of a pious forgery [illegible] vii, 6.)

Pisistratus expelled the [illegible]

[illegible] improved, in the [illegible] to the reputations of [illegible] whenever one of their [illegible] people said, "Oh, *that* [illegible] interpolations of Onoma- [illegible] was passed over. This [illegible] to have been among the [illegible] Homer under Pisistratus.[1] [illegible] repented, and, many years [illegible] into attempting his dis- [illegible] This he did by "keeping [illegible] unfavourable to the barbarians," [illegible] any that seemed favourable. [illegible] Pisistratus believed in him as [illegible] giving credit to exposed and [illegible]"

[illegible] practised deceit, it is to be [illegible] Onomacritus acquired a liking for [illegible] forgery, which, as will be [illegible] of Ireland, grows on a man [illegible] Onomacritus is generally [illegible] authorship of the poems which [illegible] attributed to Orpheus, the [illegible] Perhaps the most interest- [illegible] of Orpheus to us would have [illegible] or Κατάβασις ἐς ᾅδου, in

[illegible] editors is much disputed. The [illegible] of the Pisistratids.

which the poet gave his
descent to Hades in search
only a dubious reference to
journey is quoted by Plutarch
exact truth about the Orphic
(the reader may pursue the
quest in Lobeck's "Aglaophamus
certain that the period between
Pericles, like the Alexandrian times
age for literary forgeries. But
frauds the greatest (according to
"advanced" theory on the subject
"Forgery of the Iliad and Odyssey
opinions of the scholars who hold that
and Odyssey, which we know and
knew, are not the epics known to
but later compositions, are far from
or consistent. But it seems to be
that about the time of Pericles
kind of Greek Macpherson. This
impostor worked on old epic
added many new ideas of his own
gods, converting the Iliad (the poem
now possess) into a kind of
a Greek Don Quixote. He
number of pseudo-archaic
expressions, and added the

[1] Or, more easily, in

[illegible] unknown. It is [illegible] the sixth century. If [illegible] Paley, that the [illegible] Iliad and Odyssey were [illegible] Æschylus, and the con- [illegible] we must also suppose [illegible] invented most of [illegible] Odyssey and Iliad. Ac- [illegible] the "cooker" of the [illegible] the greatest and most [illegible] impostors, for he de- [illegible] world, from Plato downwards, [illegible] by Mr. Paley. There are [illegible] inclined to believe that Plato [illegible] the forger himself, as Bacon, [illegible] other hypothesis) was the [illegible] plays. Thus "Plato [illegible] browed Verulam," would [illegible] who" forge! Next to [illegible] imposture, no doubt, the false [illegible]" are the most important of [illegible] And these illustrate, like [illegible], the extreme worthless- [illegible] as a criterion of the [illegible] For what man ever [illegible] taste than Sir William [illegible] accomplished writer of [illegible] never thought of

without calling to mind those
Lucretius—

> Quem tu, dea, tempore
> Omnibus ornatum voluisti exc

Well, the ornate and excellent Temple
"the Epistles of Phalaris have more
spirit, more force of wit and genius
others he had ever seen, either
modern." So much for what
Temple's "Nicety of Tast." The
English scholars readily proved
used (in the spirit of prophecy) an
did not exist to write about matters
not invented, but "many centuries
he." So let the Nicety of Temple's
its absolute failure be a warning to
read (if read we must) German critics
Homer's claim to this or that
Plato's right to half his accepted
grounds of literary taste. And
Herodotus would have said, to the
Phalaris, of Socrates, of Plato;
of Pythagoras and of Homer,
other uncounted literary forgeries
world, from the Sibylline
Battle of the Frogs and Mice,

Early Christian frauds were
We have the apocryphal

[illegible] which were not
[illegible] Perhaps the most
[illegible] (if forgery be
[illegible] this case) was that of
[illegible] "Of a sudden," says
[illegible] the pontificate of Nicholas
[illegible] sudden was promulgated,
[illegible] preparation, not ab-
[illegible] but apparently over-
[illegible] doubt, a new Code, which to
[illegible] documents added fifty-nine
[illegible] of the twenty oldest Popes
[illegible] Melchiades, and the donation
[illegible] in the third part, among the
[illegible] Popes and of the Councils from
[illegible] II., thirty-nine false decrees,
[illegible] several unauthentic Councils."
[illegible] posed," Milman adds, "with
[illegible] piety and reverence." The
[illegible] naturally assert the supremacy
[illegible] Rome. "They are full and
[illegible] property" (they were sure to
[illegible] they remind one of another
[illegible] Aryan, "The Institutes of
[illegible] not levy any tax upon
[illegible] Brahman forger of the
[illegible] from the mouths of
[illegible] in a yellow robe, im-

perturbable, decorated with
while Lakshmi was stroking
soft palms." The Institutes
of Brahmans and cows, as the
the Pope and the clergy, and
had about as much hand in the
Vishnu had in his Institutes.
"Pantagruel," did well to have the
Decretals sung by *filles belles,*
cettes, et de bonne grace. And then
drank to the Decretals and their
health. "O dives Décretales, tant
le vin bon bon trouvé"—"O divine
how good you make good wine taste
miracle would be greater," said
they made bad wine taste good."
that can now be done by the
Decretals is "to palliate the guilt of
whose name, like that of the Greek
is unknown.

If the early Christian centuries
Middle Ages, were chiefly occupied
frauds, with forgeries of gospels,
Decretals, the impostors of the
busy, as an Oxford scholar said,
of a new MS. of the Greek
something really important,"
imitations. After the Turks

[illegible] scattered all over [illegible] many genuine classical [illegible] recovered by the zeal of [illegible] plays of Menander were seen [illegible] ever, it was natural that [illegible] thrive. As yet scholars [illegible] than critical; they were col- [illegible] rather than minutely [illegible] remains of classic literature. [illegible] so much, and every year were [illegible] more, that no discovery seemed [illegible] lost books of Livy and Cicero, [illegible] Sappho, the perished plays of [illegible] Æschylus might any day be [illegible] This was the very moment [illegible] forger; but it is improbable that [illegible] period has escaped detection. [illegible] years ago some one published a [illegible] the "Annals of Tacitus" were [illegible] Bracciolini. This paradox [illegible] converts than the bolder hypo- [illegible] The theory of Hardouin [illegible] ancient classics were produc- [illegible] company which worked, in [illegible] under Severus Archontius. [illegible] exceptions to his sweeping [illegible] writings were genuine, [illegible] Pliny's, of Virgil the

Georgics; the satires and epist... Herodotus, and Homer. All the ... classics were a magnificent forgery ... rate thirteenth century, which had ... Greek, and whose Latin, abundant ... in quality left much to be desired. ...

Among literary forgers, or passers ... literary coin, at the time of the Re... Annius is the most notorious. Annius ... vernacular name was Nanni) was born ... in 1432. He became a Dominican ... publishing his forged classics) rose to the ... of Maître du Palais to the Pope, ... Borgia. With Cæsar Borgia it is ... Annius was never on good terms. He ... in preaching "the sacred truth" to his ... and this (according to the detractors ... was the only use he made of the ... There is a legend that Cæsar Borgia ... the preacher (1502), but people ... that charge against Cæsar when ... any way connected with him happ... Annius wrote on the History and ... Turks, who took Constantinople ... but he is better remembered by ... tatum Variarum Volumina XVII ... Fr. Jo. Annii." These fragments ... included, among many other ...

[illegible] Rector, the pre-
[illegible] perplexed that Annius,
[illegible] did not publish choice
[illegible] lately" the ancient
[illegible] them and preserved
[illegible] Moneta. Among the
[illegible] Annius were treatises by
[illegible] Cato, and poems by Archi-
[illegible] been divided as to whether
[illegible] a knave, or whether he was
[illegible]. Or, again, whether he
[illegible] fragments, and eked them
[illegible] inventions. It is observed
[illegible] dovetail the really genuine
[illegible] and Manetho into the works
[illegible]. This may be explained as
[illegible] ignorance or of cunning; there can
[illegible] difference. "Even the Dominicans,"
[illegible] admit that Annius's discoveries
[illegible] they excuse them by averring
[illegible] was the dupe of others. But
[illegible] has been found to defend
[illegible] of the Dominican.

[illegible] remember that the great and
[illegible] taken in by some pseudo-
[illegible]. The joker of jokes was
[illegible] published, says Mr. Besant, "a
[illegible] which he proudly

called "Ex reliquiis venera consisting of a pretended will The name of the book is "Ex randæ antiquitatis. Lucii Caspidii Item contractus venditionis antiqui temporibus initus. *Lugduni apud* (1532)." Pomponius Lætus and tanus were apparently authors of the

Socrates said that he "would his hand against his father Parmenid fathers of the Church have not been fully treated by literary forgers Renaissance. The "Flowers of The St. Bernard, which were to be a *ad gaudia Paradisi* (Strasburg, really, it seems, the production of Garlande. Athanasius, his "Eleven cerning the Trinity," are attributed to a colonial Bishop in Northern Africa, false classics were two comic Latin with which Muretus beguiled Scaliger, has suffered, posthumously, from the to him of a very disreputable volume In 1583, a book on "Consolations" was published at Venice, containing tions with which Cicero consoled death of Tullia. It might as attributed to Mrs. Blimber,

[illegible] which that lady
[illegible] the affliction of never
[illegible] his Tusculan villa. The
[illegible] Sigonius, of Modena,
[illegible] discover some Ciceronian
[illegible] he was not the builder, at
[illegible] of Tully's lofty theme.
[illegible] Nodot, conceiving the world
[illegible] enough of Petronius Arbiter,
[illegible] in which he added to the
[illegible] though accomplished author.
[illegible] that he had found a whole
[illegible] at Belgrade, and he published
[illegible] of his own Latin into
[illegible] dissatisfied with the existing
[illegible] humour was Marchena, a
[illegible] books, who printed at Bâle
[illegible] edition of a new fragment.
[illegible] very cleverly inserted in a
[illegible] In spite of the ironical style
[illegible] many scholars were taken in by
[illegible] their credulity led Marchena
[illegible] (of Catullus this time) at
[illegible] Eichstadt, a Jena professor,
[illegible] that the same fragment
[illegible] the university library, and,
[illegible] various readings, cor-
[illegible] in prosody. Another

sham Catullus, by Corradino,
published in 1738.

The most famous forgeries of
century were those of Macpherson,
and Ireland. Space (fortunately)
permit a discussion of the Ossianic
That fragments of Ossianic legend
Ossianic poetry) survive in oral Gaelic
seems certain. How much Macpherson
of these, and how little he used
bombastic prose which Napoleon
spelled "Ocean"), it is next to
discover. The case of Chatterton
known to need much more than
most extraordinary poet for his years
lived began with the forgery of a
pedigree for Mr. Bergum, a pewterer
started on his career in much the
unless Ireland's "Confessions" be
a fraud, based on what he knew about
ton. Once launched in his career
drew endless stores of poetry from
MS." and the muniment chest in
Redcliffe's. Jacob Bryant believed
wrote an "Apology" for the credibility
who believed in his own system
might have believed in anything
terton sent his "discoveries"

[illegible] Gray
and Walpole,
injured, took no
Chatterton's death was
genius come to
found him wiser, and
the fatal demon of
had to find work, like
[illegible]

century, which had
by the Chatterton and
witnessed also the great
forgeries. We shall
truth about the fabrica-
documents, and
other plays. We have,
of the culprit: *habemus*
Mr. W. H. Ireland was
clerk, so versatile and
we cannot always trust him,
the tale of his own
but wide and turbu-
Ireland forgeries suggests
that criticism and
hundred years ago were)
literary touchstones. A
society, a society devoted
stage, was taken in

by a boy of eighteen. Young[illegible]
palmed off his sham prose, [illegible]
makeshift imitations of the [illegible]
his ridiculous verses on the [illegible]
Boswell went down on his knees [illegible]
Heaven for the sight of them, and [illegible]
after these devotions, drank hot [illegible]
water. Dr. Parr was not less [illegible]
and probably the experts, like [illegible]
held aloof, were as much influenced [illegible]
as by science. The whole story [illegible]
Ireland's forgeries is not only too [illegible]
told here, but forms the topic of a [illegible]
Talk of the Town") by Mr. James [illegible]
frauds in his hands lose neither their [illegible]
their complicated interest of plot. [illegible]
then, Mr. Samuel Ireland was a [illegible]
extremely fond of old literature and [illegible]
If we may trust the "Confessions" [illegible]
candid son, Mr. W. H. Ireland, a more [illegible]
and confiding old person than [illegible]
collected early English tracts. [illegible]
learned society, his son, Mr. W. [illegible]
acquired not only a passion for [illegible]
but a desire to emulate Chatterton[illegible]
step in guilt was the forgery of [illegible]
an old pamphlet, with which he [illegible]
Ireland. He also wrote a [illegible]

[illegible] represented
[illegible] that the
[illegible] this new
[illegible] Ireland con-
[illegible] unjustifiable opinion
[illegible] find merit in
[illegible] enough. Ireland's
[illegible] forgery of some legal
[illegible] Shakespeare. Just as
[illegible] the guileless Mr.
[illegible] "Deuteronomy" on the
[illegible] synagogue rolls, so young
[illegible] ends of old rent rolls,
[illegible] quantities of old fly-leaves
[illegible] ancient paper he indicted
[illegible] faith, which he attributed
[illegible] a strong "evangelical,"
[illegible] gave a very Protestant com-
[illegible] document. And still
[illegible] wondered and believed.

[illegible] to write in an ink made
[illegible] liquids used in the marbling
[illegible] binding. This stuff was
[illegible] a bookbinder's apprentice;
[illegible] questions as to whence all
[illegible] manuscripts came, he said
[illegible] by a gentleman who
[illegible] 'Finally,' the

impossibility of producing
one of the causes of the detecti
According to himself, Ireland
digies of acuteness. Once he
random, the name of a contempo
speare. He was confronted with
signature, which, of course, was
He obtained leave to consult his
gentleman," rushed home, forged
again on the model of what had be
him, and returned with this signat
gift from his benefactor. That name
had informed him (he swore) that
two persons of the same name, and
signatures were genuine. Ireland's
went the length of introducing an
his own, with the same name as him
the companions of Shakespeare. If
had succeeded (and it was actually
stage with all possible pomp), Irela
have produced a series of pseudo-Sh
plays from William the Conquer
Elizabeth. When busy with "V
was detected by a friend of his
pounced on him while he was
pounced on Onomacritus. The
ever, consented to "stand in"
did not divulge his secret

suspicion waxed so strong,
inquiries for the anonymous
numerous, that Ireland fled
house. He confessed all, and,
account, fell under the un-
Samuel Ireland. Any reader of
will be likely to sympathise
the dupe of his son. The
told with a curious mixture of
humour, and with great plausi-
Ireland admits that his "desire
was, almost irresistible, when
pompous, sagacious people—
to the papers. One feels
forgive the rogue for the sake of
cleverness, his humour. But the
not improbably, almost as
the original documents. They
the sake of money, and it is
how far the same mercenary
Ireland in his forgeries. Dr.
"Shakespeare Fabrications,"
view of the conduct, not only
of old Samuel Ireland. Sam,
Ingleby, was a partner in the
and the confession was only
the scheme of fraud. Old
of a band of young

literary Dodgers. He [illegible]
whole family to trade in [illegible]
Mr. W. H. Ireland, he was [illegible]
complished liar that ever [illegible]
certainly a distinction in its [illegible]
of the joke is that, after the [illegible]
exploded, people were anxious to [illegible]
of the forgeries. Mr. W. H. Ireland [illegible]
to the occasion. He actually forged [illegible]
(according to Dr. Ingleby) his father's [illegible]
and, by thus increasing the supply, [illegible]
the market with sham shams, with [illegible]
imitations. If this accusation be [illegible]
impossible not to admire the colossal [illegible]
of Mr. W. H. Ireland. Dr. Ingleby [illegible]
ardour of his honest indignation, [illegible]
William into his private life, which, [illegible]
was far from exemplary. But literary [illegible]
should be content with a man's [illegible]
domestic life is matter, as *Aristotle* [illegible]
"for a separate kind of investigation [illegible]
Ritson used to say that "every literary [illegible]
deserved hanging as much as a [illegible]
W. H. Ireland's merits were [illegible]
by the law.

How old Ritson would have [illegible]
old corrector," it is "better [illegible]
the wicked say, according [illegible]

[illegible] The dis-
[illegible] apocryphal old
[illegible] his misdeeds
[illegible] mind by the
[illegible] of the learned
[illegible] Payne Collier. Mr.
[illegible] mildly, the Shapira of
[illegible] brought that artist's
[illegible] but *why?* how de-
[illegible] it is once more
[illegible] Mr. Collier first in-
[illegible] notice his singular copy
[illegible] (second edition), loaded
[illegible] emendations, in 1849.
[illegible] book was simple and
[illegible] one day, to be in the
[illegible] the bookseller, in Great
[illegible] a parcel of second-hand
[illegible] the country. When the
[illegible] the heart of the Bibliophile
[illegible] packet contained two old
[illegible] an old folio Shakespeare of
[illegible] (1632). The volume (mark
[illegible]ped," greasy, and imper-
[illegible] of Mr. Hamilton's
[illegible] whole affair is already
[illegible] Mr. Collier said that
[illegible] in the possession

new Shakespearian docu
received with extreme scep
the fruit, except acres of
dence, which the world has
Collier's greasy and imperfect
rected folio."

The recency and (to a Shak
the importance of these forgeri
humble merits of Surtees, with
the "Slaying of Antony Feath
and of "Bartram's Dirge." Surte
lacunæ in these songs, "collect
tradition," and furnished notes as
they took in Sir Walter Scott,
moments when I half suspect "the
sel" (who blamelessly forged so
from "Old Plays") of having comp
mont Willie." To compare old Scott
account of Kinmont Willie with
to feel uncomfortable doubts.
rank impiety. The last ballad
note was the set of sham Macedo
popular songs (all about Alex
and other heroes) which a schoo
Rhodope imposed on M. Verko
was not badly done, and the
slang" was excellent. The
too, was successful enough

English. With this latest effort of the tenth muse, the crafty muse of Literary Forgery, we may leave a topic which could not be exhausted in a ponderous volume. We have not room even for the forged letters of Shelley, to which Mr. Browning, being taken in thereby, wrote a preface, nor for the forged letters of Mr. Ruskin, which occasionally hoax all the newspapers.

Surtees apparently forged, not only ballads, but the Latin legend of the Spectre Knight which Scott wove into "Marmion." See the author's "Old Friends," appendix.

BIBLIOMANIA IN

THE love of books for their
paper, print, binding, and for
as distinct from the love
stronger and more universal
than elsewhere in Europe.
lishers are men of business;
aspire to be artists. In England
what they read from the libraries
gaudy cloth-binding chance
them. In France people buy
them to their heart's desire
dainty devices on the morocco
are lifelong friends in that country
they are the guests of a week
The greatest French writers
of curious editions; they
treatises to the love of
and history of France
the good and bad

[illegible] disappointments. [illegible] this moment a small [illegible] books,—the "Bibliophile [illegible] large volumes, "Les Sonnets [illegible] La Bibliomanie en 1878," [illegible] d'un Bibliophile" (1885) and [illegible] works of Janin, Nodier, Beraldi, [illegible] great collectors who have written [illegible] of beginners and the pleasure [illegible] who takes delight in printed paper. [illegible] for books, like other forms of [illegible] changes of fashion. It is not [illegible] to justify the caprices of taste. [illegible] or absence of half an inch of [illegible] "uncut" margin of a book makes [illegible] of value that ranges from five [illegible] hundred pounds. Some books are [illegible] they are beautifully bound; [illegible] competed for with equal eagerness [illegible] never have been bound at all. The [illegible] make absurd mistakes about [illegible]. Some time ago the *Daily* [illegible] reproached a collector because his [illegible]," whence, argued the journa- [illegible] that he had never read them. [illegible] only means that the margins [illegible] curtailed by the binder's plough. [illegible] to like books just as they left the hands of ... Estienne, Aldus, or Louis ...

It is because the passion ... sentimental passion that people ... felt it always fail to understand ... is not an easy thing to explain ... especially find it impossible to ... and emotions that are not ... wrongs of Ireland, (till quite recently ... tions of Eastern Roumelia, the ... Greece. If we are to understand ... hunter, we must never forget that ... are, in the first place, *relics*. His ... that the great writers whom he admires ... just such pages and saw such an ... type as he now beholds. Molière ... corrected the proofs for this edition ... "Précieuses Ridicules," when he ... "what a labour it is to publish a book ... *green* (*neuf*) an author is the ... print him." Or it may be that ... turned over, with hands unstrung ... broken by the torture, these leaves ... his passionate sonnets. Here again ... of Theocritus from which ... may have read aloud to charm ... pontifical leisure of Leo X. ... the counterpart of that ...

[illegible] Master
[illegible] *ballads*, with
[illegible] hanging from one
[illegible] the "Last Dying
[illegible] François Villon."
[illegible] Eve of St. Agnes"
[illegible] Shelley doubled up
[illegible] when the prow of the
[illegible] into the timbers of the
[illegible] books have these associa-
[illegible] nearer to the authors
[illegible] reprints. Bibliophiles will
[illegible] early *readings* they care
[illegible] fancies, and those more
[illegible] which he afterwards cor-
[illegible] have their literary value,
[illegible] masterpieces of the great; but
[illegible] all is the main thing.
[illegible] to be relics in another way.
[illegible] which belonged to illustrious
[illegible] collectors who make a
[illegible] golden chain of bibliophiles)
[illegible] since printing was in-
[illegible] Grolier (1479–1565),—not a
[illegible] English newspaper supposed
[illegible] was on his travels),—
[illegible] the great Colbert, the
[illegible]), Charles Nodier,

a man of yesterday, M. Didot, and ... too numerous to name. Again, there ... books of kings, like Francis I., Henri III., ... Louis XIV. These princes had their ... devices. Nicolas Eve, Padeloup, ... other artists arrayed their books in ... tooled with skulls, cross-bones, and ... for the voluptuous pietist Henri III., with ... salamander for Francis I., and powdered ... *fleurs de lys* for the monarch who "was ... State." There are relics also of noble ... The volumes of Marguerite d'Angoulême ... covered with golden daisies. The ... Marie Antoinette adorns too many books ... Madame du Barry might have welcomed ... hastily improvised library. The three ... of Louis XV. had their favourite ... morocco, citron, red, and olive, and their ... are valued as much as if they bore the ... De Thou, or the interwined *C*'s of the ... and ridiculous Abbé Cotin, the *Trissotin* ... comedy. Surely in all these things ... human interest, and our fingers ... thrilled, as we touch these books, ... off contact of the hands of kings and ... scholars and *coquettes*, pedants, ... *cieuses*, the people who are ... mob that inhabited dead ...

[illegible] has the love of [illegible] in France, that it would [illegible] a kind of bibliomaniac [illegible] country. All her rulers, kings, [illegible] have had time to spare for [illegible] going too far back, to the [illegible] span and Charlemagne was [illegible] give a few specimens of an [illegible] history of French bibliolatry, be- [illegible] courteous, with a lady. "Can a [illegible] bibliophile?" is a question which [illegible] at the weekly breakfast party [illegible] Pixérécourt, the famous book- [illegible] playwright, the "Corneille of the [illegible] The controversy glided into a dis- [illegible] how many books a man can love [illegible] historical examples prove that [illegible] (and Italian, witness the Princess [illegible] the bibliophiles of the true strain. [illegible] was their illustrious patroness. [illegible] of Henri II. possessed, in the [illegible] a library of the first triumphs [illegible] Her taste was wide in range, [illegible] plays, romances, divinity; her [illegible] Fathers were bound in citron [illegible] with her arms and devices, [illegible] of silver. In the love of [illegible] else, Diane and Henri II.

were inseparable. The ... scattered over the covers of ... lily of France is twined ... of Diane, or round the quiver, ... the bow which she adopted ... in honour of the maiden goddess ... of Henri and of Diane remained ... d'Anet till the death of the Princess ... in 1723, when they were dispersed ... the famous Madame de Goyon ... greater part of the library, which ... scattered again and again. M. Léop... a well-known bibliophile, possess... examples.[1]

Henri III. scarcely deserves, ... name of a book-lover, for he pro... read the works which were bound ... most elaborate way. But that gre... Alexandre Dumas, takes a far ... view of the king's studies, and, in "... Monsoreau," introduces us to a lear... Whether he cared for the contents ... or not, his books are among the ... relics of a character which excite... curiosity. No more debauched ... wretch ever filled a throne; ... man in Aristotle, Henri III, ...

[1] See Essay on "...

[illegible] dancing is an un[illegible] [illegible] knees in his chapel. [illegible] books, of which an [illegible] bears his cipher and [illegible] but the centre is occupied [illegible] of the Annunciation, [illegible] the crucifixion and the [illegible] which the swords have [illegible] device was the death's- [illegible] motto *Memento Mori*, or *Spes* [illegible] he was still only Duc d'Anjou, [illegible] de Clèves, Princesse de [illegible] sudden death he expressed his [illegible] done his piety, by aid of the [illegible] bookbinder. Marie's initials [illegible] his book-covers in a chaplet [illegible] one corner a skull and cross- [illegible]; in the other the motto *Mort* [illegible] two curly objects, which did [illegible] filled up the lower corners. The [illegible] III., even when they are abso- [illegible] literature, sell for high prices; [illegible] on theology, decorated with [illegible] lately brought about £120 [illegible]

[illegible] patron of all the arts, was [illegible] of bindings. The fates of [illegible] illustrated by the story of

the copy of Homer, on
Aldus, the great Venetian
Francis I. After the death of
of Hastings, better known as
than of books, his possessions
the hammer. With the instinct,
French say, of the bibliophile,
Firmin Didot, the biographer of
that the marquis might have owned
in his line. He sent his agent over
to the country town where the
held. M. Didot had his reward.
books which were dragged out of
store-room was the very Aldine
Francis I., with part of the original
clinging to the leaves. M. Didot
precious relic, and sent it to what
(who has written a century of sonnets
mania) calls the hospital for books.

> Le dos humide, je l'éponge ;
> Où manque un coin, vite me
> Pour tous j'ai maison de santé.

M. Didot, of course, did not practise
surgery himself, but had the
of Francis I. restored by one of
binders who only work for
and Rothschilds.

During the religious wars

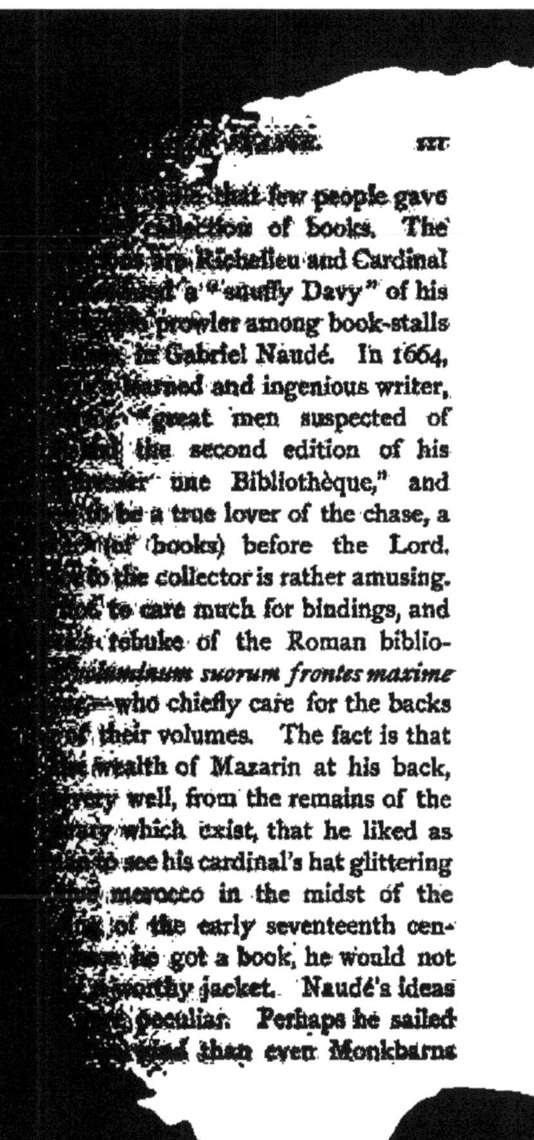

[illegible] that few people gave [illegible] collection of books. The [illegible] Richelieu and Cardinal [illegible] a "snuffy Davy" of his [illegible] prowler among book-stalls [illegible] in Gabriel Naudé. In 1664, [illegible] learned and ingenious writer, [illegible] "great men suspected of [illegible] the second edition of his [illegible] une Bibliothèque," and [illegible] to be a true lover of the chase, a [illegible] (of books) before the Lord. [illegible] to the collector is rather amusing. [illegible] to care much for bindings, and [illegible] rebuke of the Roman biblio- [illegible] *suorum frontes maxime* [illegible] who chiefly care for the backs [illegible] of their volumes. The fact is that [illegible] wealth of Mazarin at his back, [illegible] well, from the remains of the [illegible] which exist, that he liked as [illegible] to see his cardinal's hat glittering [illegible] morocco in the midst of the [illegible] of the early seventeenth cen- [illegible] he got a book, he would not [illegible] worthy jacket. Naudé's ideas [illegible] peculiar. Perhaps he sailed [illegible] than even Monkbarns would have cared to do. His favourite ... to buy up whole libraries in the gross, ... tive lots" as the dealers call them. ... second place, he advised the book-lover to ... the retreats of *Libraires fripiers, et les* ... *fonds et magasins.* Here he truly observes ... you may find rare books, *brochés,*—that ... bound and uncut,—just as Mr. Symonds ... two uncut copies of "Laon and Cythna" ... Bristol stall for a crown. "You may get ... for four or five crowns that would cost you ... or fifty elsewhere," says Naudé. Thus ... years ago M. Paul Lacroix bought for ... francs, in a Paris shop, the very copy of " ... tuffe" which had belonged to Louis XIV. ... example may now be worth perhaps £200. ... we are digressing into the pleasures of ... modern sportsman.

It was not only in second-hand book... that Naudé hunted, but among the deal... waste paper. "Thus did Poggio find ... on the counter of a wood-merchant, and ... picked up 'Agobardus' at the shop of ... who was going to use the MS. to ... books withal." Rossi, who may ... Naudé at work, tells us how he ... shop with a yard-measure in his ... books, we are sorry to say ...

[illegible] were like the towns [illegible] the Tartars had swept [illegible] *— et non hominis unius [illegible] quandam per omnes biblio- [illegible] videatur !"* Naudé [illegible] own. In 1652 the Parliament [illegible] of the splendid library [illegible] was perhaps the first free [illegible] — the first that was open to [illegible] of right of entrance. There [illegible] description of the sale, from which [illegible] will avert his eyes. On Mazarin's [illegible] he managed to collect again and [illegible] which form the germ of the [illegible] *Mazarin.*

[illegible] and popes it is pleasant to [illegible] of letters, and he the greatest of [illegible] who was a bibliophile. The [illegible] rivals of Molière—De Visé, De [illegible] the rest—are always reproaching [illegible] of *bouquins.* There is some [illegible] among philologists about [illegible] *bouquin,* but all book-hunters [illegible] of the word. The *bouquin* is [illegible] volume, black with tarnished [illegible] among the wares of the stall- [illegible] and dust, till the hunter [illegible] the quarry. We like to think of Molière lounging through the streets in the evening, returning, perhaps, from some noble house where he has been reading the proscribed "Tartuffe," or giving an imitation of the rival actors at the Hôtel Bourgogne. Absent as the *contemplateur* is, a dingy book-stall wakens him from his reverie. His lace ruffles are soiled in a moment with the dust of ancient volumes. Perhaps he picks up the only work out of all his library that is known to exist,—*un ravissant petit Elzevir*, "De Imperio Magni Mogolis" (Lugd. Bat. 1631). On the title-page of this tiny volume, one of the series of "Republics" which the Elzevirs published, the poet has written his rare signature, "J. B. P. Molière," with the price the book cost him, "1 livre, 10 sols." "Il n'est pas de bouquin qui s'échappe de ses mains," says the author of "La Guerre Comique," the last of the pamphlets which flew about during the great literary quarrel about "L'École des Femmes." Thanks to M. Soulié the catalogue of Molière's library has been found, though the books themselves have passed out of view. There are about three hundred and fifty volumes in the inventory. Molière's widow may have omitted some (it is the foible of her sex) many books now worth far more than their weight

[illegible] than two hundred and
[illegible] French and Italian comedies,
[illegible] what suited him wherever
[illegible] had plenty of classics, histories,
[illegible] the essays of Montaigne,
[illegible] Bible.

[illegible] to the regret of bibliophiles,
[illegible] in bindings. Did he have a
[illegible] stamped on the leather (that device
[illegible] plate), or did he display his
[illegible] arms, the two apes that support
[illegible] with three mirrors of Truth?
[illegible] Bruyère tells us as much—that
[illegible] of book-lover in the seventeenth
[illegible] the same sort of person as his
[illegible] own time. "A man tells me
[illegible] says La Bruyère (*De la Mode*);
[illegible] to see it. I go to visit my
[illegible] receives me in a house where,
[illegible] the smell of the black morocco
[illegible] books are covered is so strong
[illegible] He does his best to revive
[illegible] ear that the volumes 'have
[illegible] they are 'elegantly tooled,' that
[illegible] good edition,' . . . and informs
[illegible] reads' that 'he never sets
[illegible] his house,' that he 'will come
[illegible] him for all his kindness,

and have no more desire than
tanner's shop that he calls his library.

Colbert, the great minister of
a bibliophile at whom perhaps La
have sneered. He was a collector
read, but who amassed
looked forward, as business men do
when he should have time to study
Grolier, De Thou, and Mazarin,
sessed probably the richest private
Europe. The ambassadors of
charged to procure him rare books
scripts, and it is said that in a
with the Porte he inserted a clause
a certain quantity of Levant
use of the royal bookbinders.
days, had no literature with
deigned to be acquainted. Even
however, valuable books had been
and we find Colbert pressing the
sador at St. James's to bid for him
sale of rare heretical writings.
wanted to gain his favour
presents of books, and the city of
two real curiosities—the famous
and the Missal of Charles
Elzevirs sent him their
though Colbert probably

VENETIIS, ALDUS, 1559.

than of their contents, at
and handed down many
As much may be said for the
Dubois, who, with all his
collector. Bossuet, on the other
little or nothing of interest except a
edition of Molière, whom he
condemned to "the punishment of
laugh." Even this book, which has
interest, has slipped out of sight, and
ceased to exist.

and Dubois preserved books from
there are collectors enough who
rescued from oblivion by books. The
of D'Hoym is forgotten; the plays
Longepierre, and his quarrels with J. B.
are known only to the literary his-
These great amateurs have secured an
of gilt edges, an immortality of morocco.
prices are given for any trash that
them, and the writer of this notice
for four shillings an Elzevir classic,
it bears the golden fleece of Longe-
worth about £100. Longepierre,
and the Duc de la Vallière,
are less interesting to us
and Loque, the neglected
They found some pale

consolation in their little cabinets ... their various liveries of olive, citron ... morocco.

A lady amateur of high (book-collecting) reputation, the Comtesse de Verrue, was represented in the Beckford sale by one of ... copies of "L'Histoire de Mélusine," of M... the twy-formed fairy, and ancestress of the ... of Lusignan. The Comtesse de Verrue ... the few women who have really ... book-collecting,[1] was born January 18, 16... died November 18, 1736. She was the daughter of Charles de Luynes and of his second ... Anne de Rohan. When only thirteen ... married the Comte de Verrue, who some... injudiciously presented her, a *fleur de gal...* as Ronsard says, at the court of Victor Am... of Savoy. It is thought that the countess ... less cruel than the *fleur Angevine* of Ro... For some reason the young matron fled ... the court of Turin and returned to Paris ... she built a magnificent hotel, and received ... most distinguished company. According ... biographer, the countess loved science ... *jusqu'au délire*, and she collected the ... of the period, without neglecting the ... of the glowing Orient. ...

[1] See Essay in "Lady ...

[illegible] thousand volumes,
[illegible] artists of the day.
[illegible] the present, without fear of
[illegible] pursuing the beautiful,
[illegible] with a tender heart and open
[illegible] passed through life, calm,
[illegible] and admired." She left an
[illegible] thus rudely translated :—

[illegible] in sleep secure,
[illegible] inclined to mirth,
Who, by way of making sure,
Chose her Paradise on earth.

[illegible] Revolution, to like well-bound
[illegible] much as to proclaim one an
[illegible] might have escaped the
[illegible] had only thrown away the neat
[illegible] from the royal press, which
[illegible] for, no true Republican, but an
[illegible] The great libraries from the
[illegible] nobles were scattered among
[illegible] True sons of freedom tore
[illegible] with their gilded crests and
[illegible] revolutionary writer declared,
[illegible] not far wrong, that the art
[illegible] the worst enemy of reading,
[illegible] his studies by breaking the
[illegible] he was about to attack.
[illegible] in those sad years took

flight to England, and was kept al robust rather than refined, like Thoma Roger Payne. These were evil days, wh binder had to cut the aristocratic coat out of a book cover, and glue in a gi liberty, as in a volume in an Oxford collection.

When Napoleon became Emperor, he in vain to make the troubled and feveris of his power produce a literature. He hi was one of the most voracious readers of that ever lived. He was always asking fo newest of the new, and, unfortunately, ev new romances of his period were hopeless Barbier, his librarian, had orders to send of fresh fiction to his majesty whereve might happen to be, and great loads of followed Napoleon to Germany, Spain, Russia. The conqueror was very hard to He read in his travelling carriage, and skimming a few pages, would throw a that bored him out of the window into highway. He might have been tracked trail of romances, as was Hop-o'-my-Thu the fairy tale, by the white stones he behind him. Poor Barbier, who, pitie a passion for novels that demand volumes a day, was at his wits' e

[illegible] circumstances of the
[illegible] Napoleon had
[illegible] refused, with imperial
[illegible] again. He ordered a
[illegible] three thousand volumes to
[illegible] it was proved that the task
[illegible] accomplished in less than six
[illegible] if only fifty copies of each
[illegible] printed, would have amounted
[illegible] million francs. A Roman
[illegible] have allowed these con-
[illegible] in his way; but Napoleon,
[illegible] modern. He contented himself
[illegible] of books conveniently small in
[illegible] in sumptuous cases. The
[illegible] of France could never content
[illegible] from Moscow, in 1812, he
[illegible] clamorous for new books, and
[illegible] before they could have
[illegible], Napoleon was flying home-
[illegible] and Bennigsen.

[illegible] last of the book-lovers who
[illegible] The Duc d'Aumale, a famous
[illegible] "came to his own," and of
[illegible] known that his devotional
[illegible] found its way into the
[illegible] the era of private
[illegible] three libraries

in his time, but never a Virgil; and of Pixérécourt, the dramatist, who founded the Société des Bibliophiles Français. The Romantic movement in French literature brought in some new fashions in book-hunting. The original editions of Ronsard, Des Portes, Belleau, and Du Bellay became invaluable; while the writings of Gautier, Petrus Borel, and others excited the passion of collectors. Pixérécourt was a believer in the works of the Elzevirs. On one occasion, when he was outbid by a friend at an auction, he cried passionately, "I shall have that book at your sale!" and, the other poor bibliophile soon falling into a decline and dying, Pixérécourt got the volume which he so much desired. The superstitious might have been excused for crediting him with the gift of *jettatura*,—of the evil eye. On Pixérécourt himself the evil eye fell at last; his theatre, the Gaieté, was burned down in 1835, and his creditors intended to impound his beloved books. The bibliophile hastily packed them in boxes, and conveyed them in two cabs, and under cover of night, to the house of M. Paul Lacroix. There they languished in exile till the affairs of the manager were settled.

Pixérécourt and Nodier, the most reckless of men, were the leaders of the older school of

... was not a rich man;
... but he never hesitated to
... that he could not afford. He
... himself in the accumulation
... would recover his fortunes
... books. Nodier passed through
... Virgil, because he never succeeded
... ideal Virgil of his *dreams*,—a
... copy of the right Elzevir edition,
... and the two passages in red
... this failure was a judgment on
... by which he beguiled a certain
... Bibles. He *invented* an edition, and
... on the scent, which he followed
... died of the sickness of hope de-

... more sympathy with the eccentrici-
... than with the mere extravagance
... *haute école* of bibliomaniacs, the
... millionaires, royal dukes, and Roths-
... amateurs are reckless of prices,
... competition have made it almost
... poor man to buy a precious
... the Americans, the public
... all up in the auctions. A
... Brunet's little volume,
... 1878," will prove the ex-
... commit. The funeral

oration of Bossuet over Henriette France (1669), and Henriette Anne of (1670), quarto, in the original binding, for £200. It is true that this copy had belonged to Bossuet himself, and certain his nephew. There is an example, as we seen, of the 1682 edition of Molière,—of whom Bossuet detested,—which also belong to the eagle of Meaux. The manuscript of the divine on the work of the poor must be edifying, and in the interests of it is to be hoped that this book may come into the market. While pamphlets Bossuet are sold so dear, the first edition Homer—the beautiful edition of 1488, which three young Florentine gentlemen publish may be had for £100. Yet even that expensive, when we remember that the in the library of George III. cost only shillings. This exquisite Homer, sacred memory of learned friendships, the chief of early printing at the altar of ancient is really one of the most interesting the world. Yet this Homer is less valued the tiny octavo which contains the *huitains* of the scamp François Vil "The History of the Holy *du Sainct Gréaal*: Paris,

[illegible] Louis XIV., is [illegible] of [illegible] was treasured even in the [illegible] *[illegible]*, when old French [illegible] much despised, is certainly [illegible] Rabelais of Madame de [illegible] seems comparatively [illegible] There is something piquant in [illegible] from that famous beauty [illegible] colossal genius of Rabelais.[1]

[illegible] sympathy of collectors "to middle [illegible] is not with the rich men whose [illegible] resembles the *battue*. We [illegible] poor hunters of the wild game, [illegible] the fourpenny stalls on the *quais*, [illegible] the dusty boxes after literary [illegible] devoted men rise betimes, and [illegible] before the common tide of [illegible] by. Early morning is the best [illegible] as in other sports. At half-past [illegible] the *bouquiniste*, the dealer in [illegible] second-hand, arrays the books [illegible] over night, the stray posses- [illegible] the outcasts of libraries. [illegible] bookseller knew little of the

[illegible] Madame Pompadour's binding see over- [illegible] Rabelais in calf, lately to be seen in a

value of his wares; it was his ... small certain profit on his ... reckoned that an energetic, ... bookseller will turn over 150,000 ... year. In this vast number there ... ings for the humble collector who ... to encounter the children of Israel ... or at the Hôtel Drouot.

Let the enthusiast, in conclusion ... handful of lilies on the grave of ... the love of books,—the poet Albert ... Poor Glatigny was the son of a ... his education was accidental, and ... taste and skill extraordinarily fine ... In his life of starvation (he had often ... omnibuses and railway stations), he ... spent the price of a dinner on a new ... lived to read and to dream, and ... books he had not the wherewithal to ... he bought them,—and he died! His ... were beautifully printed by Lemerre, ... be a joy to him, if he knows it, that ... now so highly valued that the price ... would have kept the author alive and ... a month.

BINDING WITH THE ARMS OF MADAME DE POMPADOUR.

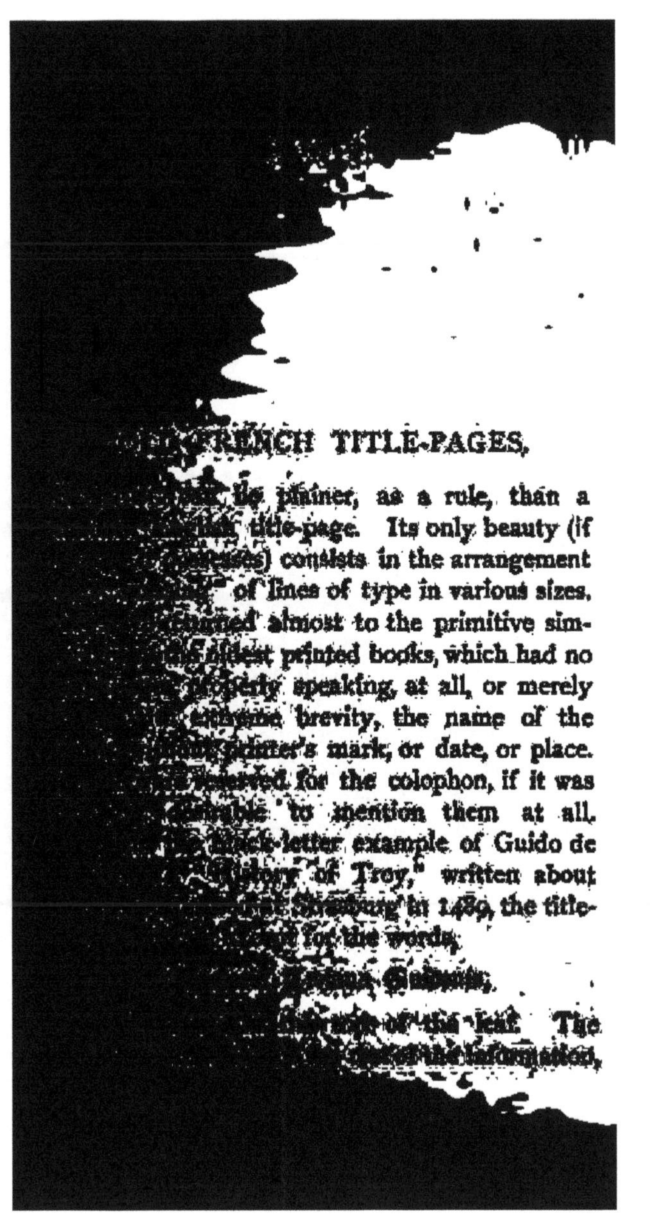

FRENCH TITLE-PAGES.

[illegible] be plainer, as a rule, than a [illegible] title-page. Its only beauty (if [illegible]) consists in the arrangement [illegible] of lines of type in various sizes. [illegible] returned almost to the primitive sim-[illegible] oldest printed books, which had no [illegible] properly speaking, at all, or merely [illegible] extreme brevity, the name of the [illegible] printer's mark, or date, or place. [illegible] reserved for the colophon, if it was [illegible] desirable to mention them at all. [illegible] black-letter example of Guido de [illegible] "History of Troy," written about [illegible] at Strasburg in 1489, the title-[illegible] for the words,

[illegible]

[illegible] side of the leaf. The [illegible] the information,

"happily completed in the
the year of Grace Mcccclxxxix,
of St. Urban." The printer and
no name at all.

This early simplicity is succeeded
books, from, say, 1510, and afterwards
insertion either of the printer's trade
black-letter books, of a rough wood
tive of the nature of the volume.
have occasionally a rude kind of
touch of the classical taste of the
sance surviving in extreme decay.
example is the title-page of "Les
d'amours, avec les responses joyeuses
by Jacques Moderne, at Lyon, 1540.
a certain Pagan breadth and joyous
figure of Amor, and the man in the
sembles traditional portraits of Dante.

There is more humour, and a good
skill, in the title-page of a book on late
and their discomforts, "Les dicts et
de trop Tard marié" (Jacques Moderne
1540), where we see the elderly and
couple sitting gravely under their

Jacques Moderne was a printer
these quaint devices, and used
his books: for example in "
God Bacchus accuse the

LEs demandes damours auec les respõses ioyeuses

Demãde respon∫e.

K

the wine," Bacchus and Satan (exactly like each other, as Sir Wilfrid Lawson will not be surprised to hear) are encouraging dishonest tavern-

Les dictz ⁊ complainctes de trop Tard marie.

keepers to stew in their own juice in a caldron over a huge fire. From the same popular publisher came a little tract on various modes of sport, if the name of sport can be applied to the

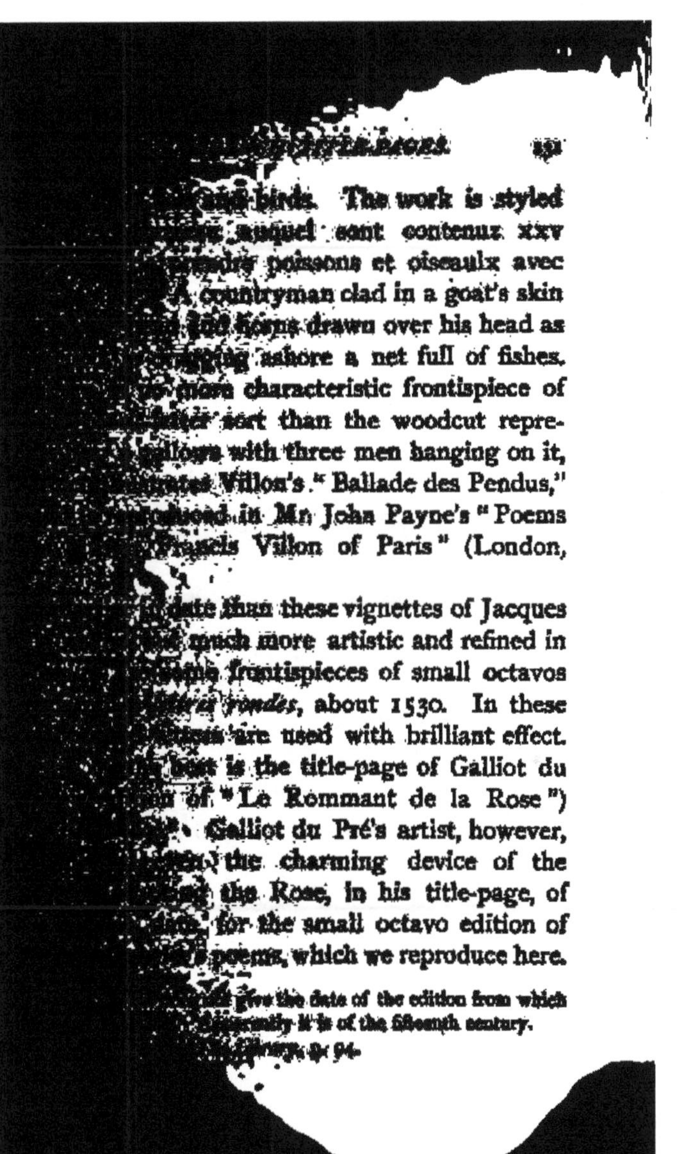

[illegible] and birds. The work is styled [illegible] auquel sont contenuz xxv [illegible] poissons et oiseaulx avec [illegible] A countryman clad in a goat's skin [illegible] horns drawn over his head as [illegible] ashore a net full of fishes. [illegible] more characteristic frontispiece of [illegible] sort than the woodcut repre- [illegible] gallows with three men hanging on it, [illegible] Villon's "Ballade des Pendus," [illegible] in Mr. John Payne's "Poems [illegible] Francis Villon of Paris" (London, [illegible]

[illegible] date than these vignettes of Jacques [illegible] much more artistic and refined in [illegible] frontispieces of small octavos [illegible] *rondés*, about 1530. In these [illegible] are used with brilliant effect. [illegible] best is the title-page of Galliot du [illegible] of "Le Rommant de la Rose") [illegible] Galliot du Pré's artist, however, [illegible] the charming device of the [illegible] the Rose, in his title-page, of [illegible] for the small octavo edition of [illegible] poems, which we reproduce here.

[illegible] give the date of the edition from which [illegible] it is of the fifteenth century.

[illegible] 94.

The arrangement of letters, and the use of red, make a charming frame, as it were, to the

LES OEVVRES
feu maiſtre Alain chartier en ſon
viuant Secretaire du feu roy Charles ſeptieſme du non. Nouuelle-
ment imprimees reueues &
corrigiees oultre les pre
cedētes impreſſions.

On les vend a Paris en la grant
ſalle du palais au premier Pillier en
la bouticque de Galliot du pre Li-
braire iure de Luniuerſite.
1 5 2 9

drawing of the mediæval ship, with the motto VOGUE LA GALEE.

Title-pages like these, with designs appro-

LE PASTISSIER FRANÇOIS.

Où est enseigné la maniere de faire toute sorte de Pastisserie, tres-utile à toute sorte de personnes.

ENSEMBLE

Le moyen d'aprester toutes sortes d'œufs pour les jours maigres & autres, en plus de soixante façons.

A AMSTERDAM.
Chez Louys & Daniel Elzevier.
A MDCLV.

priate to the character of the ... seded presently by the fashion ... and mottoes. As courtiers and ... private badges, not hereditary, ... personal—the crescent of Diane, ... of Francis I., the skulls and crossbones ... III., the *marguerites* of Marguerite, ... like the *Le Banny de liesse*, *Le* ... *voies périlleuses*, *Tout par Soulas*, ... so printers and authors had their ... and their private literary slogans. ... changed, according to fancy, or the ... of their lives. Clément Marot's motto ... *Mort n'y Mord.* It is indicated by ... L. M. N. M. in the curious title of an ... Marot's works published at Lyons ... Tournes in 1579. The portrait ... poet when the tide of years had borne ... from his youth, far from *L'Adolescence* ... *tine.*

The unfortunate Etienne Dolet, ... only publisher who was ever burned, ... ominous device, a trunk of a tree, ... struck into it. In publishing "Les ... de la Marguerite des Princesses, ... Royne de Navarre," Jean de Tournes ... a pretty allegorical fancy. Love ... bandage thrust back from his ...

LE
PASTISSIER
FRANCOIS
A Amſterdam,
Chez Louys et Daniel Elzevier A. 1655.

the bow and arrows in his hand,
the sun, which he seems to
metheus in the myth when
a shower of flowers and flames
Groueleau, of Paris, had for
frotte, with the thistle for
beautifully combined in the
version of Apuleius, "L'Amour de
Psyche" (Paris, 1557). There is
better date for frontispieces, both for
of device and for elegance of
title, than the years between
By 1562, when the first edition of
Fifth Book of Rabelais was
printers appear to have thought
on popular books, and the title of
posthumous chapters is printed

In 1532–35 there was a more
taste—witness the title of "Gargantua,
beautiful title decorates the first known
with a date of the First Book of
was sold, most appropriately, *devant*
de Confort. Why should so
the Master have been carried
at the Sunderland sale? All the
François Juste's Lyons editions
on this model. By 1542 he
work of architectural design.

GARGANTVA.

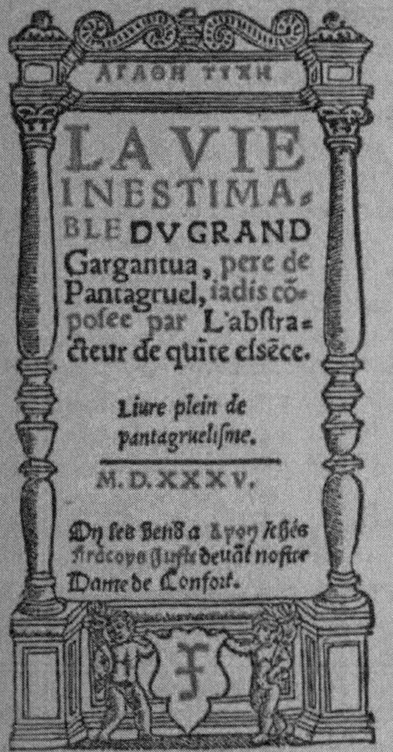
ΑΓΑΘΗ ΤΥΧΗ

LA VIE INESTIMABLE DV GRAND Gargantua, pere de Pantagruel, iadis cõposee par L'abstracteur de quīte essēce.

Liure plein de pantagruelisme.

M.D.XXXV.

On les vend a Lyon chés Frãcoys Juste devãt nostre Dame de Confort.

Breton, in Paris, was printing [illegible] a frontispiece of a classical dame [illegible] heart to the sun, a figure which [illegible] taste of Stothard, or Flaxman [illegible]

The taste for vignettes, engraved [illegible] not on wood, was revived under [illegible] Their pretty little frontispieces are [illegible] known but that we offer examples [illegible] essay on the Elzevirs in this volume [illegible] found a copy of the vignette of the [illegible] Christi," and of "Le Pastissier [illegible] reproduction is given here (pp. 133, [illegible] artists they employed had plenty of [illegible] backed by very profound skill in design [illegible]

In the same *genre* as the big-wigged [illegible] of the Elzevir vignettes, in an age [illegible] XIV. and Molière (in tragedy) [illegible] wreaths over vast perruques, are [illegible] frontispieces of Molière's own editions [illegible] Probably the most interesting of [illegible] title-pages are those drawn by Chauveau [illegible] two volumes "Les Oeuvres de M. [illegible] published in 1666 by Guillaume [illegible] The first shows Molière in two [illegible] Mascarille, and as Sganarelle [illegible] Imaginaire." Contrast the full [illegible] the *fourbum imperator*, in his [illegible] and wig, and vast *canons*, and [illegible]

LES
OEVVRES DE
Mr
MOLIERE
TOME I.

tie, with the lean melancholy of ... relle. These are two notable ... genius of the great comedian. ... are the supporters of his scutcheon...

The second volume shows ... Comedy crowning Mlle. de Molière (... Béjart) in the dress of Agnès, while ... is in the costume, apparently, of ... of Sganarelle in "L'Ecole des ... "Tartuffe" had not yet been licens... public stage. The interest of the por... costumes makes these frontispieces prec... are historical documents rather tha... curiosities.

These title-pages of Molière are ... water mark of French taste in this ... decoration. In the old quarto first ... Corneille's early plays, such as "Le C... 1637), the printers used lax and spra... binations of flowers and fruit. The... better executed, were the staple of ... Luynes, Quinet, and the other P... sellers who, one after another, failed ... Molière as publishers. The basket ... the title-page of "Iphigénie," ... (Barbin, Paris, 1675), is almost ... identical with the similar ... Visé's "La Cocue Imaginaire...

Molière's plays appearing first, small octavo, were adorned with illustrative of some scene in the in the "Misanthrope" (Ribou, Alceste, green ribbons and all, with Philinte, or perhaps listening sonnet of Oronte; it is not easy certain, but the expression of face looks rather as if he were being a sonnet. From the close of the century onwards, the taste for declined, except when Moreau or vignettes on copper, with abun- cupids and nymphs. These were for very luxurious and expensive others, men contented themselves simplicity, which has prevailed till In recent years the employment devices has been less unusual and Thus Poulet Malassis had his a chicken very uncomfortably rail. In England we have the of Messrs. Macmillan, the Trees Knowledge of Messrs. Kegan Paul the Ship, which was the sign of early place of business, and symbols, all capable of being title-page.

A BOOKMAN'S PURGA[illegible]

THOMAS BLINTON was a book-[illegible]
had always been a book-hunter, [illegible]
an extremely early age, he had [illegible]
the errors of his ways as a collector [illegible]
and monograms. In book-hunting [illegible]
harm; nay, he would contrast [illegible]
rather pharisaical style, with the [illegible]
shooting and fishing. He constant[illegible]
to believe that the devil came for th[illegible]
amateur of black letter, G. Steeven[illegible]
himself, who tells the story [illegible]
anxiety and alarm), pretends to [illegible]
the ghastly narrative. "His lang[illegible]
Dibdin, in his account of the book[illegible]
"was, too frequently, the language [illegible]
tion." This is rather good, as if [illegible]
a gentleman might swear [illegible]
"*too* frequently." "Although [illegible]
to admit," Dibdin goes [illegible]

[illegible] the good woman who watched by [illegible] bedside, although my prejudices (as [illegible] called) will not allow me to believe [illegible] shook, and that strange noises [illegible] groans were heard at midnight in his [illegible] no creature of common sense (and [illegible] possessed the quality in an eminent [illegible] mistake oaths for prayers;" and [illegible] In short, Dibdin clearly holds that [illegible] did shake "without a blast," like [illegible] in Branxholme Hall when some- [illegible] for the Goblin Page.

[illegible] Blinton would hear of none of [illegible]. He said that his taste made him [illegible]; that he walked from the City to [illegible] every day, to beat the covers [illegible] stalls, while other men travelled in [illegible] cab or the unwholesome Metro- [illegible] Railway. We are all apt to hold [illegible] views of our own amusements, and, [illegible] part, I believe that trout and salmon [illegible] of feeling pain. But the flimsi- [illegible] theories must be apparent to [illegible] moralist. His "harmless taste" [illegible] most of the deadly sins, or at all [illegible] majority of them. He [illegible] books. When he got [illegible] books in a cheap market

and sold them in a
grading literature to the
took advantage of the ignorance
persons who kept book-stalls
and grudged the good fortune
he rejoiced in their failures.
ear to the appeals of poverty.
urious, and laid out more money
have done on his selfish pleasures
ing a volume with a morocco
Mrs. Blinton sighed in vain for
d'Alençon lace. Greedy, proud,
extravagant, and sharp in his dealings
was guilty of most of the sins which
recognises as "deadly."

On the very day before that of
affecting history is now to be told,
been running the usual round of
had (as far as intentions went)
bookseller in Holywell Street by
from him, for the sum of two shillings
took to be a very rare Elzevir.
when he got home and consulted
found that he had got hold of the
in which the figures denoting the
pages are printed right, and
worth exactly "suppence"
But the intention is the

[illegible] fraudulent. When he [illegible] then "his language," as [illegible] that of imprecation." Worse [illegible] this, Blinton had gone to a [illegible] bid for "Les Essais de Michel, [illegible] Montaigne" (Foppens, MDCLIX.), [illegible] away by excitement, had "plunged" [illegible] of £15, which was precisely the [illegible] money he owed his plumber and [illegible] worthy man with a large family. [illegible] a friend (if the book-hunter has [illegible] rather an accomplice in lawless [illegible] Blinton had remarked the glee on [illegible] face. The poor man had purchased [illegible] Olaus Magnus, with woodcuts, repre-[illegible] were-wolves, fire-drakes, and other [illegible] fowl, and was happy in his bargain. [illegible] with fiendish joy, pointed out to [illegible] index was imperfect, and left him [illegible]

[illegible] foul have yet to be told. Thomas [illegible] discovered a new sin, so to speak, [illegible] way. Aristophanes says of one [illegible] blackguards, "Not only is he a [illegible] has invented an original villainy." [illegible] this. He maintained that [illegible] to notoriety had, at some [illegible] volume of poems which he had afterwards repented of [illegible] was Blinton's hideous pleasure [illegible] copies of these unhappy volumes [illegible] de Jeunesse," which, always [illegible] bear a gushing inscription from [illegible] friend. He had all Lord John [illegible] poems, and even Mr. Ruskin's [illegible] "Ode to Despair" of Smith (present [illegible] writer), and the "Love Lyrics" of [illegible] is now a permanent under-secretary, [illegible] nothing can be less gay nor more [illegible] He had the amatory songs which a dig[illegible] the Church published and withdrew [illegible] lation. Blinton was wont to say he [illegible] to come across "Triolets of a Tribune" [illegible] John Bright, and "Original Hymns [illegible] Minds," by Mr. Henry Labouchere, if [illegible] hunted long enough.

On the day of which I speak he [illegible] a volume of love-poems which the [illegible] done his best to destroy, and he [illegible] his club and read all the funnie[illegible] aloud to friends of the author, wh[illegible] club committee. Ah, was this [illegible] In short, Blinton had filled up the [illegible] iniquities, and nobody will be [illegible] that he met the appropriate [illegible] offence. Blinton had passed [illegible]

[illegible]withstanding the error about the [illegible]. He dined well at his club, went home, [illegible] and started next morning for his [illegible] the City, walking, as usual, and intend[illegible] the pleasures of the chase at all [illegible]stalls. At the very first, in the [illegible] Road, he saw a man turning over [illegible] in the cheap box. Blinton stared [illegible] fancied he knew him, thought he didn't, [illegible] became a prey to the glittering eye of [illegible]. The Stranger, who wore the con[illegible] cloak and slouched soft hat of [illegible] was apparently an accomplished [illegible], or thought-reader, or adept, or [illegible] Buddhist. He resembled Mr. Isaacs, [illegible] (in the novel of that name), Mendoza [illegible] "Coningsby"), the soul-less man in "A [illegible] Story," Mr. Home, Mr. Irving Bishop, [illegible] adept in the astral body, and most [illegible] mysterious characters of history and [illegible]. Before his Awful Will, Blinton's mere [illegible] obstinacy shrank back like a child [illegible]. The Stranger glided to him and [illegible] "Buy these."

[illegible] were a complete set of Auerbach's [illegible], which, I need not say, Blinton [illegible] dreamt of purchasing had he [illegible] devices.

"Buy these!" repeated the
ever he was, in a cruel whisper
sum demanded, and trailing
German romance, poor Blinton
fiend.

They reached a stall where, among
trash, Glatigny's "Jour de l'An
was exposed.

"Look," said Blinton, "there is a
wanted some time. Glatignys are getting
scarce, and it is an amusing trifle."

"Nay, buy *that*," said the implacable
pointing with a hooked forefinger
"History of Europe," in an indefinite
of volumes. Blinton shuddered.

"What, buy *that*, and why? In
name, what could I do with it?"

"Buy it," repeated the persecutor,
(indicating the "Ilios" of Dr. Schliemann
bulky work), "and *these*" (pointing
Theodore Alois Buckley's translation
Classics), "and *these*" (glancing at the
writings of the late Mr. Hain Friswell
"Life," in more than one volume
stone).

The miserable Blinton, paid,
along carrying the bargains
Now one book fell out,

[illegible] way. Sometimes a portion of Alison [illegible] ponderously to earth; sometimes the [illegible] Life" sank resignedly to the ground. [illegible] kept picking them up again, and [illegible] them under the arms of the weary [illegible]

[illegible] victim now attempted to put on an air [illegible], and tried to enter into conversation [illegible] his tormentor.

[illegible] know about books," thought Blinton, [illegible] must have a weak spot somewhere."

[illegible] the wretched amateur made play in his [illegible] conversational style. He talked of bind- [illegible] of Maioli, of Grolier, of De Thou, of Derome, [illegible] Clovis Eve, of Roger Payne, of Trautz, and [illegible] of Bauzonnet. He discoursed of first [illegible], of black letter, and even of illustrations [illegible] vignettes. He approached the topic of [illegible] but here his tyrant, with a fierce yet [illegible] glance, interrupted him.

[illegible] those!" he hissed through his teeth.

[illegible]" were the complete publications of [illegible] Lore Society.

[illegible] did not care for folk lore (very bad [illegible] but he had to act as he was told. [illegible] pause or remorse, he was [illegible] the "Ethics" of Aristotle, [illegible] of Williams and Chase.

Next he secured "Strathmore," ... "Under Two Flags," and "Two ... Shoes," and several dozens more ... novels. The next stall was entirely ... school-books, old geographies, Livy, ... Arnold's "Greek Exercises," Ollendorff ... what not.

"Buy them all," hissed the fiend. ... whole boxes, and piled them on Blinton ...

He tied up Ouida's novels in ... with string, and fastened each to ... buttons above the tails of Blinton's coat ...

"You are tired?" asked the ... "Never mind, these books will soon be ... hands."

So speaking, the Stranger, with ... speed, hurried Blinton back through ... Street, along the Strand, and up to ... stopping at last at the door of Blinton's ... and very expensive binder.

The binder opened his eyes, as well ... at the vision of Blinton's treasures. ... miserable Blinton found himself ... automatically and without any ... will, speaking thus :—

"Here are some things I have ... extremely rare,—and you will, ... binding them in your best manner ...

[illegible] of course ; crushed levant [illegible] every book of them, *petits fers*, [illegible] coat of arms, plenty of gilding. [illegible] Don't keep me waiting, as you [illegible]" for indeed bookbinders are the [illegible] of the human species.

[illegible] the astonished binder could ask the [illegible] questions, Blinton's tormentor [illegible] that amateur out of the room.

"[illegible] on to the sale," he cried.

"What sale ?" said Blinton.

"Why, the Beckford sale ; it is the thirteenth [illegible] lucky day."

"[illegible] I have forgotten my catalogue."

"Where is it ?"

"In the third shelf from the top, on the right-[illegible] side of the ebony book-case at home."

[illegible] stranger stretched out his arm, which [illegible] elongated itself till the hand disappeared [illegible] round the corner. In a moment the [illegible] returned with the catalogue. The pair sped [illegible] Messrs. Sotheby's auction-rooms in Wel-[illegible] Street. Every one knows the appearance [illegible] book-sale. The long table, surrounded [illegible] bidders, resembles from a little distance [illegible] and communicates the same [illegible]. The amateur is at a loss to [illegible] himself. If he bids in his

own person, some bookselle
partly because the booksell
all, he knows little about
that the amateur may, in this
Besides, professionals always
and, in this game, they have
advantage. Blinton knew all this
the habit of giving his commissions
But now he felt (and very naturally
demon had entered into him. "Tirante
Valorosissimo Cavaliere" was being
for, an excessively rare romance of
magnificent red Venetian morocco, from
vari's library. The book is one of the
the Venetian Press, and beautifully
with Canevari's device,—a simple and
affair in gold and colours. "Apollo is
his chariot across the green waves tow
rock, on which winged Pegasus is
ground," though why this action of
should be called "pawing" (the anima
ously not possessing paws) it is hard
Round this graceful design is the
ΟΡΘΩΣ ΚΑΙ ΜΗ ΛΟΞΙΩΣ. ("
crooked"). In his ordinary mood
only have admired "Tirante il
distance. But now, the demon
he rushed into the lists and

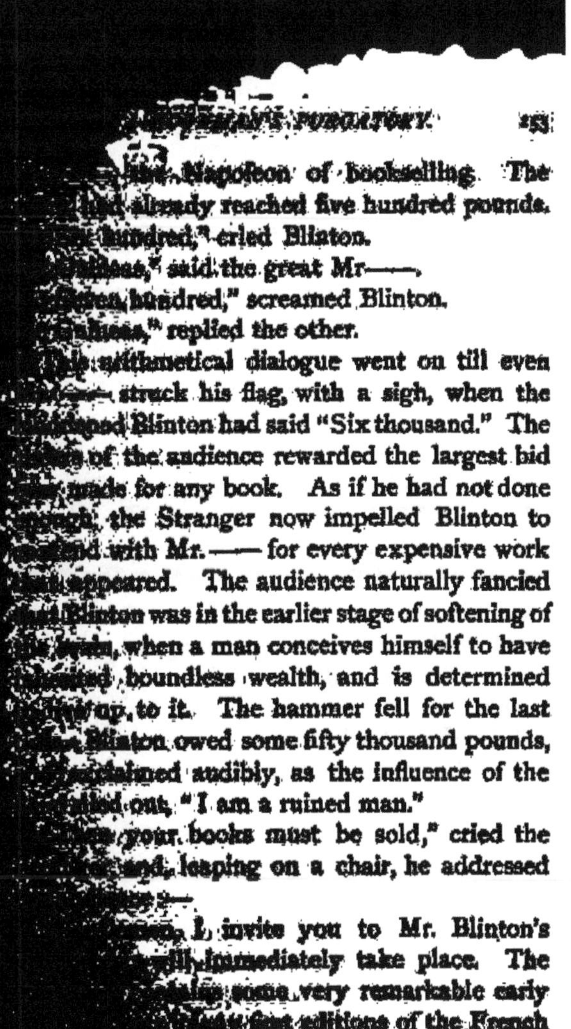

[illegible] Napoleon of bookselling. The [illegible] already reached five hundred pounds.
"[illegible] hundred," cried Blinton.
"[illegible] guineas," said the great Mr——.
"[illegible] hundred," screamed Blinton.
"[illegible] guineas," replied the other.

This arithmetical dialogue went on till even [illegible]—— struck his flag, with a sigh, when the [illegible] Blinton had said "Six thousand." The [illegible] of the audience rewarded the largest bid [illegible] made for any book. As if he had not done enough, the Stranger now impelled Blinton to [illegible] with Mr. —— for every expensive work [illegible] appeared. The audience naturally fancied [illegible] Blinton was in the earlier stage of softening of the brain, when a man conceives himself to have [illegible] boundless wealth, and is determined [illegible] up to it. The hammer fell for the last [illegible] Blinton owed some fifty thousand pounds, [illegible] exclaimed audibly, as the influence of the [illegible] out, "I am a ruined man."

"[illegible] your books must be sold," cried the [illegible] and, leaping on a chair, he addressed [illegible]:—

"[illegible], I invite you to Mr. Blinton's [illegible] will immediately take place. The [illegible] some very remarkable early [illegible] first editions of the French

classics, most of the rarer Aldines, ...
assortment of Americana ...

In a moment, as if by magic ...
round the room were filled with Blinton's ...
all tied up in big lots of some ...
each. His early Molières were ...
French dictionaries and school-books ...
Shakespeare quartos were in the ...
tattered railway novels. His copy ...
unique) of Richard Barnfield's much ...
tionate Shepheard" was coupled ...
volumes of "Chips from a German W...
and a cheap, imperfect example ...
Brown's School-Days." Hookes's "...
was at the bottom of a lot of Ameri...
tional works, where it kept company ...
Elzevir Tacitus and the Aldine "H...
machia." The auctioneer put up lot ...
and Blinton plainly saw that the ...
was a "knock-out." His most treasu...
were parted with at the price of waste ...
is an awful thing to be present at ...
sale. No man would bid above a ...
Well did Blinton know that after the ...
the plunder would be shared among ...
bidders. At last his "Adonais," ...
by Lortic, went, in company ...
"Bradshaws," the "Court Guide" ...

...lumes of the "Sunday at Home," for ...). The Stranger smiled a smile of ... malignity. Blinton leaped up to pro... the room seemed to shake around him, ... words would not come to his lips.

... he heard a familiar voice observe, as a familiar grasp shook his shoulder,—

"Tom, Tom, what a nightmare you are enjoying!"

He was in his own arm-chair, where he had fallen asleep after dinner, and Mrs. Blinton was doing her best to arouse him from his awful vision. Beside him lay "L'Enfer du Bibliophile, ... décrit par Charles Asselineau." (Paris: ..., MDCCCLX.)

* * * * * *

If this were an ordinary tract, I should have ... tell how Blinton's eyes were opened, how he gave up book-collecting, and took to gardening, ... politics, or something of that sort. But truth compels me to admit that Blinton's repentance had vanished by the end of the week, when he ... discovered marking M. Claudin's catalogue, ...ly, before breakfast. Thus, indeed, ... remorses. "Lancelot falls to his ...," as in the romance. Much, and ... decry a death-bed repent... the only repentance that we do not repent of. All others leave us ready, when occasion comes, to fall to our old love again; and may that love never be worse than the taste for old books! Once a collector, always a collector. *Moi qui parle*, I have sinned, and struggled, and fallen. I have thrown catalogues, unopened, into the waste-paper basket. I have withheld my feet from the paths that lead to Sotheby's and to Puttick's. I have crossed the street to avoid a book-stall. In fact, like the prophet Nicholas, "I have been known to be steady for weeks at a time." And then the fatal moment of temptation has arrived, and I have succumbed to the soft seductions of Eisen, or Cochin, or an old book on Angling. Probably Grolier was thinking of such weaknesses when he chose his devices *Tanquam Ventus*, and *quisque suos patimur Manes*. Like the wind we are blown about, and, like the people in the Æneid, we are obliged to suffer the consequences of our own extravagance.

BALLADE OF THE UNATTAINABLE.

THE Books I cannot hope to buy,
Their phantoms round me waltz and wheel,
They pass before the dreaming eye,
Ere Sleep the dreaming eye can seal.
A kind of literary reel
They dance; how fair the bindings shine!
Prose cannot tell them what I feel,—
The Books that never can be mine!

There frisk Editions rare and shy,
Morocco clad from head to heel;
Shakespearian quartos; Comedy
As first she flashed from Richard Steele;
And quaint De Foe on Mrs. Veal;
And, lord of landing net and line,
Old Izaak with his fishing creel,—
The Books that never can be mine!

Incunables! for you I sigh,
Black letter, at thy founts I kneel,
Old tales of Perrault's nursery,
For you I'd go without a meal!
For Books wherein did Aldus deal
And rare Galliot du Pré I pine.
The watches of the night reveal
The Books that never can be mine!

ENVOY.

Prince, hear a hopeless Bard's appeal;
Reverse the rules of Mine and Thine;
Make it legitimate to steal
The Books that never can be mine!

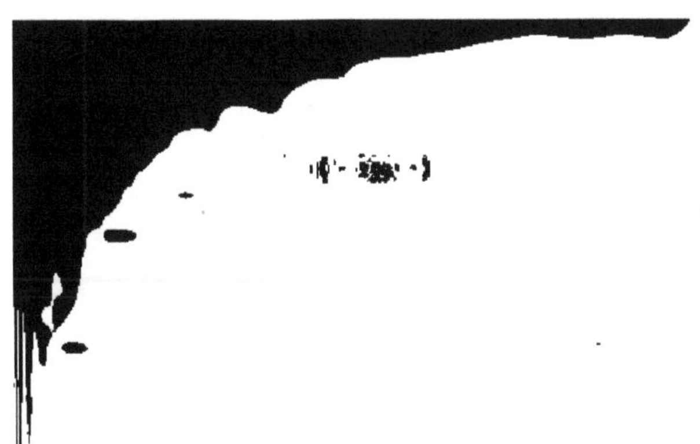

LADY BOOK-LOVERS.

THE biographer of Mrs. Aphra Behn refutes the vulgar error that "a Dutchman cannot love." Whether or not a lady can love books is a question that may not be so readily settled. Mr. Ernest Quentin Bauchart has contributed to the discussion of this problem by publishing a bibliography, in two quarto volumes, of books which have been in the libraries of famous beauties of old, queens and princesses of France. There can be no doubt that these ladies were possessors of exquisite printed books and manuscripts wonderfully bound, but it remains uncertain whether the owners, as a rule, were bibliophiles; whether their hearts were with their treasures. Incredible as it may seem to [illegible] literature was highly respected in the [illegible] even fashionable. Poets were in [illegible] and Fashion decided that the [illegible] books, and not only books,

but books produced in the
art, and bound with all the
of Clovis Eve, and Padeloup
Therefore, as Fashion gave her
cannot hastily affirm that the ladies
were really book-lovers. In our
age, Fashion has decreed that ladies
and bet, and romp, but it would
to assert that all ladies who do
these matters are born romps, or
affected liking for cigarettes. History
maintains that many of the
whose books are now the most
literary relics were actually inclined
well as to pleasure, like Marguerite
and the Comtesse de Verrue, and
de Pompadour. Probably books
more to this lady's liking than the
which she beguiled the tedium of
and many a time she would rather
quiet with her plays and novels than
conscientiously conducted but

Like a true Frenchman, M.
written about French lady book-
women who, like Mary Stuart,
half French. Nor would it
English author to name,
crowned heads, like

[illegible] who has a passion for the [illegible] of literature for binding, and first [illegible] large paper, and engravings in [illegible]. The practical sex, when studious, [illegible] same sex when fond of equestrian [illegible]. "A lady says, 'My heyes, he's an [illegible] and he must go,'" according to Leech's [illegible]. In the same way, a studious girl or [illegible] says, "This is a book," and reads it, if [illegible] she does, without caring about the date, or the state, or the publisher's name, or even [illegible] often about the author's. I remember, [illegible] the publication of a novel now celebrated, [illegible] a privately printed vellum-bound copy on [illegible] in the hands of a literary lady. She [illegible] it over the fire, and had already [illegible] the vellum covers curl wide open like the [illegible] of an afflicted oyster. When I asked [illegible] the volume was, she explained that "It is [illegible] which a poor man has written, and he's [illegible] to see whether some one won't be [illegible] to publish it." I ventured, perhaps [illegible] to point out that the poor man [illegible] very poor, or he would not have [illegible] experiment on Dutch paper. [illegible] did not know how that [illegible] feeling the expert [illegible] contempt for [illegible]

everything but the spi[illegible]
there is an aversion to [illegible]
display of morocco and [illegible]
which amuse the minds of [illegible]
have caught "the Bibliom[illegible]
have taken this pretty fever [illegible]
But it must be owned that the [illegible]
possessed, being rarer and more [illegible]
even more highly prized by [illegible]
examples from the libraries of [illegible]
Longepierre, and D'Hoym. M. [illegible]
is a complete guide to the colle[illegible]
expensive relics. He begins his [illegible]
women who have owned books [illegible]
of the Valois, Marguerite d'Angoul[illegible]
of Francis I. The remains of [illegible]
chiefly devotional manuscripts. [illegible]
be noted that all these ladies, [illegible]
possessed the most devout and [illegible]
whole collections of prayers [illegible]
pen, and decorated with [illegible]
guerite's library was bound in [illegible]
with a crowned M in *interlac*[illegible]
or, at least, with conventional [illegible]
may have been meant for [illegible]
choose, perhaps the most [illegible]
mens extant is "La [illegible]
des Poëtes, Homère," [illegible]

[illegible] translation Ronsard writes a prologue, addressed to the manes of Salel, in which he complains that he is ridiculed for his poetry. He draws a characteristic picture of Homer and Salel in Elysium, among the learned lovers:

> qui parmi les fleurs devisent
> Au giron de leur dame.

Marguerite's manuscript copy of the First Book of the Iliad is a small quarto, adorned with daisies, fleurs de-lis, and the crowned M. It is in the Duc d'Aumale's collection at Chantilly. The books of Diane de Poitiers are more numerous and more famous. When first a widow she stamped her volumes with a laurel springing from a tomb, and the motto, "Sola vivit in illo." But when she consoled herself with Henri II. she suppressed the tomb, and made the motto meaningless. Her crescent shone not only on her books, but on the palace walls of France, in the Louvre, Fontainebleau, and Anet; and her initial D. is inextricably blended with the H. of her royal lover. [illegible] Henri added the D to his own cypher, [illegible] have been so embarrassing for his [illegible] that people have good-naturedly [illegible] the curves of the D's as C's. The [illegible] and the bows of his Diana [illegible] the covers of Henri's

Book of Hours. Catherine's ... double C enlaced with an ... (Katherine) combined in ... These, unlike the D.H., are ... a crown—the one advantage ... possessed over the favourite. ... books are various treatises on ... surgery, and plenty of poetry and ... Among the books exhibited ... Museum in glass cases is ... Bembo's "History of Venice." ... collector, Mr. Barlow, of New York ... enough to possess her "Singularitez ... Antarctique" (Antwerp, 1558).

Catherine de Medicis got splendid ... the same terms as foreign pirates ... English novels—she stole them. ... Strozzi, dying in the French service ... collection, on which Catherine laid ... Brantôme says that Strozzi's son ... to him a candid opinion about this ... What with her own collection and ... the Marshal's, Catherine possessed ... thousand volumes. On her death ... peril of being seized by her ... almoner carried them to ... Thou had them placed ... Unluckily, it was ...

[illegible] with Catherine's compromis-[illegible] her creditors should single them [illegible] take them away in their pockets. [illegible] books with her arms and cyphes are [illegible] rare.[1] At the sale of the collections of the Duchesse de Berry, a Book of Hours of [illegible] was sold for £2400.

Mary Stuart of Scotland was one of the lady book-lovers whose taste was more than a mere following of the fashion. Some of her books, like one of Marie Antoinette's, were the companions of her captivity, and still bear the sad complaints which she entrusted to these last friends of fallen royalty. Her note-book, in which she wrote her Latin prose exercises when a girl, still survives, bound in red morocco, with the arms of France. In a Book of Hours, now the property of the Czar, may be partly deciphered the quatrains which she composed in [illegible] years, but many of them are [illegible] by the binder's shears. The Queen [illegible] as a kind of album: it contains [illegible] of the "Countess of Schrewsbury" [illegible] has it), of Walsingham, of the [illegible] and of Charles Howard, Earl of [illegible] There is also the signature, "Your [illegible] Seymour;" and

This remarkable
in Paris, during the
browsky, who carried
Book of Hours of the
scription, in a
sont les Heures de
guerite de Blacuod de
it is not very easy to
Marguerite was probably the
Blackwood, who wrote a
Stuart's sufferings (Edinburgh

The famous Marguerite de
Henri IV., had certainly a
many beautifully bound books
daisies are attributed to her
bear the motto, "Expectata
appears to refer, first to the
which is punctual in the
"the constellated flower
next, to the lady, who will
is the lady Marguerite de
books have been sold at
relics of the leman of La
possible to demonstrate
her shelves, that they
ing from her own

[illegible] they form a most important collection, [illegible]ally bound; science and philosophy in citron morocco, the poets in green, and history and theology in red. In any case it is absurd to explain "Expectata non eludet" as a reference to the lily of the royal arms, which appears on the centre of the daisy-pied volumes. The motto, in that case, would run, "Expectata (lilia) non eludent." As it stands, the feminine adjective, "expectata," in the singular, must apply either to the lady who owned the volumes, or to the "Margarita," her emblem, or to both. Yet the ungrammatical rendering is that which M. Bouchot suggests. Many of the books, Marguerite's or not, were sold at prices over £100 in London, in 1884 and 1883. The Macrobius, and Theocritus, and Homer are in the Cracherode collection at the British Museum. The daisy-crowned Ronsard went for £430 at the Beckford sale. These prices will probably never be reached again.

[illegible] Anne of Austria, the mother of Louis XIV., [illegible] a bibliophile; she may be suspected of acting [illegible] motive, "Love me, love my books." [illegible] affection for Cardinal Mazarin there [illegible] doubt: the Cardinal had a [illegible] and his royal friend probably [illegible] In her time, and on her volumes, the originality [illegible] binder, Le Gascon, began [illegible] The fashionable passion for [illegible] Fontaine made such sacrifices, [illegible] of book decoration, and Le [illegible] patterns of gold points and [illegible] the productions of Venice. The [illegible] books include many devotional [illegible] whatever other fashions might [illegible] piety was always constant [illegible] tion. Anne of Austria seems [illegible] particularly fond of the lives and [illegible] Theresa, and Saint François de Sales [illegible] of the Cross. But she was not [illegible] old French poets, such as Coquillart [illegible] descended to Ariosto; she had [illegible] character, Théophile de Viau [illegible] bound; she owned the Rabelais [illegible] what is particularly interesting, M. [illegible] possesses her copy of "L'Eschole [illegible] Comédie par J. B. P. Molière. [illegible] de Luynes, 1663." In 12°, [illegible] edges, and the Queen's arms [illegible] This relic is especially valuable [illegible] member that "L'Ecole [illegible] Arnolphe's sermon to Agnès [illegible] threats of future punishment [illegible] take the form of [illegible]

[illegible] was often appealed to by [illegible] Molière, yet Anne of Austria [illegible] seen his comedy, but possessed [illegible] example of the first edition. M. [illegible] Lacroix supposes that this copy was offered [illegible] Queen-Mother by Molière himself. The [illegible] (Arnolphe preaching to Agnès) is [illegible] to be a portrait of Molière, but in the [illegible]duction in M. Louis Lacour's edition it is [illegible] to see any resemblance. Apparently [illegible] did not share the views, even in her later [illegible] of the converted Prince de Conty, for [illegible] comedies and novels remain stamped [illegible] her arms and device.

[illegible] learned Marquise de Rambouillet, the [illegible] of all the "Précieuses," must have owned [illegible] library, but nothing is chronicled save [illegible] celebrated book of prayers and meditations, [illegible] out and decorated by Jarry. It is bound [illegible] morocco, *doublé* with green, and covered [illegible] in gold. The Marquise composed the [illegible] for her own use, and Jarry was so much [illegible] their beauty that he asked leave to [illegible] into the Book of Hours which [illegible] the prayers are often so [illegible] that I am ashamed to write

[illegible] of the devotions which

jarry admired, a prayer [illegible]
published in "Miscellanies [illegible]
M. Prosper Blanchemain: [illegible]

PRIÈRE À SAINT[illegible]

ROY DE FRANCE[illegible]

Grand Roy, bien que votre couronne [illegible] esclatantes de la Terre, celle que vous [illegible] incomparablement plus précieuse. [illegible] l'autre est immortelle et ces lys dont [illegible] ternir, sont maintenant incorruptibles. [illegible] vostre mère; vostre justice envers vos [illegible] contre les infideles, vous ont acquis la [illegible] peuples; et la France doit à vos travaux [illegible] l'inestimable tresor de la sanglante et [illegible] Sauveur du monde. Priez-le incomparable[illegible] une paix perpetuëlle au Royaume dont [illegible] sceptre; qu'il le préserve d'hérésie; qu'il [illegible] saintement vostre illustre Sang; et que [illegible] l'honneur d'en descendre soient pour jamais [illegible]

The daughter of the Marquise, [illegible] heroine of that "long courtship [illegible] Montausier, survives in these [illegible] possessor of "La Guirlande de Julie [illegible] script book of poems by eminent [illegible] this manuscript seems to have [illegible] library of Julie; therein she [illegible] read of her own perfections [illegible] had also "L'Histoire de [illegible] hero for whom, like [illegible]

[illegible] in supreme devotion. In the "Guirlande," Chapelain's verses turn on the pleasing fancy that the Protestant Lion of the North, changed into a flower (like Paul Limayrac in M. Banville's ode), requests Julie to take pity on his altered estate:

> Sois pitoyable à ma langueur;
> Et si je n'ay place en ton cœur
> Que je l'aye au moins sur ta teste.

These verses were reckoned consummate.

The "Guirlande" is still, with happier fate than attends most books, in the hands of the successors of the Duc and Duchesse de Montausier.

Like Julie, Madame de Maintenon was a *précieuse*, but she never had time to form a regular library. Her books, however, were bound by Duseuil, a binder immortal in the verse of Pope; or it might be more correct to say that Madame de Maintenon's own books are hardly distinguishable from those of her favourite foundation, St. Cyr. The most interesting is a copy of the first edition of "Esther," in quarto (1689), bound in red [illegible] and bearing, in Racine's hand, "*A [illegible] la Marquise de Maintenon, offert avec [illegible].*"

[illegible] had the book bound before

he presented it. [illegible]
writes his son Louis, [illegible]
in a simple marbled paper [illegible]
that this worthy custom [illegible]
sake of the art of binding [illegible]
amateur poets would be [illegible]
presentation copies. It is [illegible]
turn these gifts with their [illegible]
inner walls of bookcases, to be [illegible]
the damp, but the trouble [illegible]
worthless presents from [illegible]
siderable.[1]

Another interesting example [illegible]
Maintenon's collections is Dacier's [illegible]
Critiques sur les Œuvres d'Horace [illegible]
arms of Louis XIV., but with his [illegible]
on the fly-leaf (1681).

Of Madame de Montespan, [illegible]
royal favour by Madame de [illegible]
"married into the family [illegible]
governess," there survives one [illegible]
interest. This is "Œuvres [illegible]
auteur de sept ans," in quarto [illegible]
printed on vellum, and with [illegible]
mother of the little Duc [illegible]
When Madame de Maintenon [illegible]

[1] Country papers, [illegible]

[illegible] for the children of the king and of [illegible] de Montespan, she printed those [illegible] of her eldest pupil.

[illegible] ladies were only bibliophiles by accident, [illegible] devoted, in the first place, to pleasure, [illegible] or ambition. With the Comtesse de [illegible], whose epitaph will be found on an [illegible] page, we come to a genuine and even [illegible] collector. Madame de Verrue (1670-[illegible]) got every kind of diversion out of life, [illegible] when she ceased to be young and fair, she turned to the joys of "shopping." In early [illegible], "pleine de cœur, elle le donna sans compter." In later life, she purchased, or obtained on credit, everything that caught her [illegible], also *sans compter*. "My aunt," says the Duc de Luynes, "was always buying, and never [illegible] her fancy." Pictures, books, coins, [illegible] engravings, gems (over 8,000), tapestries, [illegible] furniture were all alike precious to Madame [illegible]. Her snuff-boxes defied computa[illegible] had them in gold, in tortoise-shell, in [illegible] lacquer, and in jasper, and she [illegible] delicate fragrance of sixty different [illegible] without applauding the smoking [illegible] drawing-rooms, we may admit [illegible] than steady applications to [illegible]

The Countess had a noble library, for old tastes survived in her commodious heart, and new tastes she anticipated. She possessed "The Romance of the Rose," and "Villon," in editions of Galliot du Pré (1529–1533) undeterred by the satire of Boileau. She had examples of the "Pleïade," though they were not again admired in France till 1830. She was also in the most modern fashion of to-day, for she had the beautiful quarto of La Fontaine's "Contes," and Bouchier's illustrated Molière (large paper). And, what I envy her more, she had Perrault's "Fairy Tales," in blue morocco—the blue rose of the folklorist who is also a book-hunter. It must also be confessed that Madame de Verrue had a large number of books such as are usually kept under lock and key, books which her heirs did not care to expose at the sale of her library. Once I myself (*moi chétif*) owned a novel in blue morocco, which had been in the collection of Madame de Verrue. In her old age this exemplary woman invented a peculiarly comfortable arm-chair, which, like her novels, was covered with citron and violet morocco; the nails were of silver. If Madame de Verrue has met the Baroness Bernstein, their conversation in the Elysian Fields must be of the most gallant and interesting description.

[illegible] literary lady of pleasure, Madame de Pompadour, can only be spoken of with modified approval. Her great fault was that she did not check the decadence of taste and sense in the art of bookbinding. In her time came in the habit of binding books (if binding it can be called) with flat backs, without exhibiting the sinews that are of the very essence of book-covers. Without showing these no binding can be orthodox, nor in the best and most legitimate manner. It is very deeply to be deplored that by far the most accomplished living English artist in bookbinding has reverted to this old and most dangerous heresy. The most original and graceful tooling is of much less real value than naturalness, and a book bound with a flat back can hardly be said to be properly bound at all. The practice was the herald of the French and may open the way for the English Revolution. Of what avail were the ingenious [illegible] of Derome to stem the tide of change, [illegible] books whose sides they adorned were [illegible] flat-backed. Madame de Pompadour's [illegible] were of all sorts, from the inevitable [illegible] to devotions of another sort, [illegible] of Erycina Ridens. One of [illegible] singular fortunes, a copy of [illegible] with the Regent's illustrations, and those of Cochin [illegible] quarto, 1757, red morocco, [illegible] adorned with billing and cooing doves [illegible] arrows of Eros, with burning hearts, [illegible] and shepherds. Eighteen years ago this [illegible] was bought for ten francs in a [illegible] Hungary. A bookseller gave £8 for [illegible] M. Bauchart paid for it £150; and [illegible] left his shelves, probably he too made [illegible] bargain. Madame de Pompadour's "Apology for Herodotus" (La Haye, 1735) has [illegible] legend. It belonged to M. Paillet, who [illegible] a glorified copy of the "Pastissier François" [illegible] M. Bauchart's collection. M. Paillet [illegible] it, with a number of others, for the "Pastissier" [illegible]

> J'avais "L'Apologie
> Pour Hérodote," en reliûre ancienne, [illegible]
> De livre provenant de chez la Pompadour,
> Il me le soutira![1]

Of Marie Antoinette, with whose [illegible] book-lovers of the old *régime* must [illegible] survive many books. She had a library [illegible] Tuileries, as well as at le petit T[illegible] her great and varied collections [illegible] valued as her little book of [illegible] her consolation in the [illegible]

[illegible]

in the Temple and the Conciergerie. The book is "Office de la Divine Providence" (Paris, 1757, green morocco). On the fly-leaf the Queen wrote, some hours before her death, these touching lines: "*Ce* 16 *Octobre, à* 4 *h.* ½ *du matin. Mon Dieu! ayez pitié de moi! Mes yeux n'ont plus de larmes pour prier pour vous, mes pauvres enfants. Adieu, adieu!*—MARIE ANTOINETTE."

There can be no sadder relic of a greater sorrow, and the last consolation of the Queen did not escape the French popular genius for cruelty and insult. The arms on the covers of the prayer book have been cut out by some fanatic of Equality and Fraternity.

THE END.

PRINTED BY WILLIAM CLOWES AND SONS, LIMITED, LONDON AND BECCLES.

Lightning Source UK Ltd.
Milton Keynes UK
UKHW020939180821
388974UK00002B/253